Spiritual Runner:
A Runner After God's
Own Heart

Sophie, Read this! And Be inspired to be all that God has created you to be.! I love you!
M.

Jolee Paden

ISBN: 978-1-60383-494-0

Published by:
Holy Fire Publishing
www.ChristianPublish.com

Printed in the United States of America and the United Kingdom

Course Map

Intro

Devotionals

Conclusion

"Step on the course acting like it is the most important thing, knowing that it is not."
- Coach Jason Lewkowicz

Intro

Preface

My journey began with a prayer for an opportunity. An opportunity begins with surrendering and finding a passion to share with others. You must decide to submit yourself to something beyond yourself and your own control.

After I asked for an opportunity, God began to open doors and I was amazed at the abundance of opportunities that were put before me when I offered myself sacrificially to the mission of the kingdom.

Spiritual Runner was one of those opportunities. Over time, a vision became clear: runners have the power to change Christianity and the box that the church has been put in. We are a demonstration of the kingdom! We know about suffering, victory, self-discipline, community and sacrifice! We have an opportunity to change the way people see Christianity, because I believe we understand Christianity in a way that Jesus intended it to be understood.

*   *   *

After struggling through my first year of college cross country and track with some medical issues, the last race of my season was the 10K on the track. This was the first time that I had ever run the 10K...on the track. Twenty-five laps. For the first time in my life, the goal was simply to finish the race.

I ran in last for a while (of all 9 girls crazy enough of to run the race). It was extremely humbling, yet I just wanted to make it through and finish strong. I ran alongside two other girls for quite a while and I encouraged them. My encouragement might have been a personal pep talk more than anything.

The last lap arrived and with a pang of wild energy like I have never experienced before, I took off. If there is one moment in which I have ever felt the glory of God while running, that was it. There was such freedom. There wasn't first place victory as I crossed the line as the seventh place finisher, but there was still such a beautiful feeling of victory.

After I finished the race I saw one of my competitors who I had ran with for most of the race. I went up to her to simply tell her she did a great job. We talked for a little bit. As she shared some of her heart with me, I felt this knocking on my heart to pray for her. This is not something I had ever done before, but it sprouted up and I seized the opportunity to pray over her.

As I cooled down alone on the track, I never felt so humbled while feeling so alive in Christ. He empowered me to do his work on the track that night. I would have liked to win, but he knew right where he wanted me.

It was in the last couple laps of my cool down that I had this thought: What if Jesus ran track? Sounds silly, right? I remember giggling to myself as I thought it. But is it really that far-fetched? Shouldn't we be proclaiming the brilliance of Jesus in our actions and our speech everywhere we go...even on the track?

I imagined this awesome picture of Jesus gathering around with his opponents and encouraging them, praying for them, telling them the goodness of the Gospel and seeking out the broken. One of my favorite parts of this picture was what it would be like if Jesus began speaking in parables to a group of runners. He would use running analogies in order to relate to his people, so they could grasp the life-changing message of living in his kingdom. That may sound silly too, but that is what he was doing during his lifetime as he used farming parables along with a multitude of other stories. He did this because the people would understand.

Running is so real for us. For many it is a lifestyle, often turned obsession. Our emotions run parallel with our weekly mileage and workouts while we carve out hours for training. Yet it is so hard to spend a mere five minutes with the Lord in prayer and seeking his will in his Word.

OUR PRIORITIES ARE SKEWED.

Do not be confused to think that running is bad. No way! Running can be a beautiful act of worship when it is used to glorify our God as we utilize our talents. We get ourselves in trouble when we put the god of running above our God of grace, love, and mercy. Or when we believe we can equate the two and make them co-pilots in our life as if they determine our future circumstances, joys, and disappointments.

Distance runners have a hard time of admitting defeat, just like anyone else. We have worked too hard and too long to not be the best, right? But that is where we are wrong. We do not deserve one bit of our grit because none of it is ours to begin with. It is time to surrender our strengths in pursuit of a victory far greater than a shiny trophy or medal.

We have the unique opportunity to serve the Lord in success and defeat and it is always good. Are you ready for everlasting joy regardless of your circumstances? Sounds too easy?

Don't worry it will be quite the workout.

Changing the Way We Compete

What does it mean to compete for Christ? So often we hear, "Glory to God," but what does that mean for the way we live, run and compete?

1. We are seeking to conform to the image of Christ and his teaching. Christ gave everything he had to bring glory back to God. He let go of all selfish ambitions or situational anxiety and submitted it all to God. He became obedient to death, even death of a cross (Philippians 4).

2. So what does it look like to give everything we have to offer when we live and when we train and compete? God is honored when we submit all we have for not our own personal glory, but for his glory.

   We must renounce the hardship of the circumstances. When Christ was carrying his cross through the streets of Jerusalem, do you think there was time to complain? No, he sought the Lord and lived to only please him despite his discomfort.

3. We are competing for an Audience of One. God's view of us is the only one that matters. Why do we get stuck trying to compare ourselves to others or appear impressive? Because that is our world! But we are not of this world or the flesh— we serve God who is higher than anything else. By giving your all so God is the only judge of your performance, you are competing for an Audience of One. There is such freedom in this! There is freedom to make mistakes with no fear of condemnation (Romans 8:1). If you put everything you have to give on the course, there is nothing more to do. God created you and He knows what he created you to do. Honor him in worship by offering your body and talents as a living sacrifice.

When you begin competing for Christ, it is no longer about what *you* can do, but what Christ can do through you. It is not about how much you are honored, but how much honor God is gaining by serving him with our best.

Encouragement should no longer take root in "You can do it" but "Who is working through you?" and "Who is empowering you?" The Scriptures act as our motivator because "if God is for us, who can be against us?" (Romans 8:31)

Devo Navigation

There are a couple of ways to use this devotional. Anyway you do it, two purposes should be served. The first is to read the Bible. The second is to take the devo challenges, prayers, verse meditations and reflections into your daily life and races in order to learn what it means to conform to the image of Christ.

Begin by reading the Scripture and then go on to read the devotional material. Then, go back to the Scripture and read it again. I would suggest reading more of the context of the Scripture to really dig into the Word and see what God has for you. The more you are able to read and understand, the better!

Start your quiet time in prayer asking God to reveal the lesson he has for you as you meditate on his Word. Enter into his presence with an air of thankfulness. Offer your heart up to God: your praises and your concerns. Allow his Word to transform you into who you were created to be in him. In a journal or blank book sections, write your thoughts and prayers to God the Father.

I have also added in some stories and daily training thoughts to add variety to your devotional experience. It is important to keep things fresh!

* A Bible will be necessary for going through these devotionals. If you have a smart phone or smart device, download a Bible App for free! If that does not work, contact your local church and ask them to hook you up with a book of God's Word!

Devotionals

Worship | Psalm 86:9-10

When you hear the word "worship," do you imagine singing at a church service? Sure, this is one way to worship, but we have the opportunity to worship God in everything we do and everything we are.

As runners, we can worship God through our running. What does that look like though?

Just like God gave someone a beautiful voice to sing in church, God gave you an incredible talent to run. As believers, we are to use the gifts God has given us to reach all corners of his kingdom and make the most of what we have been given. First, we must see that our ability is from God alone and without him we have nothing.

Running as worship means completely removing yourself from the task at hand and offering yourself to God. Removing yourself from running sounds impossible. While it is difficult, it is not impossible. Live in mindfulness of the gift of God's freedom and the sacrifice of his Son. If someone sang in front of the church always thinking of themselves and their talent, there would be a disconnect in worship. We have a role of connection to play between believers, non-believers and everyone in between when we run with our eyes fixed on Jesus Christ and the ultimate goal of his message.

God, I praise you for the ability to run. Forgive me for taking advantage of this gift you have given me. I recognize that you have given me this ability for a specific reason and I refuse to let it go to waste. As I learn what it means to worship in my running, help me to seek and find you in all that I do for my life should be worship. While it is hard to get through my head sometimes, I thank you for being the sovereign God of all.

Rom. 12:1 offering our bodies as living sacrifices — holy + pleasing to God — this is our spiritual worship

-3

Discipline | Hebrews 12:7-14

Runners pour discipline into their daily lives to educate, edify and improve their training. Dedicating yourself to a lifestyle of small disciplines like not quitting when you are tired, builds a strong mind and body for the future. We see the value in discipline. While it is not always enjoyable in the moment, we remind ourselves of the end reward or goal.

As discipline in training continues, you begin to embrace the difficulties for you keep your eyes on your ultimate purpose. For those who do not have goals or an understanding of their purpose, it is challenging to continue disciplining themselves. Individuals can become lazy and complacent when they do not have their goal in sight.

Similarly, those who do not have their goal in sight (serving the Lord through loving him and others), find it difficult to discipline themselves. They forget where their treasure is being stored. Is it being stored in the glory of heaven or the depths of the earth?

When you stay focused, you begin to see the benefits of learning the nature of Jesus as you read the Bible, pray, serve and fellowship with other believers. Just like in your physical training, there will be tough days but the beauty of the outcome is plentiful: love and freedom. The instinct of living like Jesus will take over without you having to search so deeply. You will realize how essential your spiritual training is to life.

God, thank you for helping me see the value of discipline in my daily life so I can apply it in my relationship with you. Forgive me for the days that I seek discipline in my training, but neglect to seek discipline in my relationship with you. Remind me the importance of godliness over bodily training. Also, remind me of whom you created me to be as I serve you and love your people like you love me.

1 Tim 4:8

" For physical training is of some value, but godliness has value for ALL THINGS, holding promise for our present life + life to come "

4

John 14:15
If you love me you will obey
what I command!

Fruit | John 15:1-17

I want to be faster. I hope and pray every day that I will become faster. I don't have much motivation besides just wanting to be faster. Eventually, I start getting angry and I don't make much progress.

I want to be more patient. I hope and pray every day that I will be more patient. I don't have much motivation besides just wanting to be more patient. Eventually, I start getting angry and I don't make much progress.

How often do you wish you were more loving, joyful, peaceful, patient, kind, good, faithful, or self-controlled (See Galatians 5:22-23)? Have you ever found yourself praying to have more of any of these characteristics?

These are called fruit of the Spirit for a reason. Fruit is a product of a tree. When one wants to grow fruit on a tree, it cannot be done by going out and wishing there was fruit on the tree. Even if you went out and stared at the branches where the fruit should grow, it would never sprout life. You have to attend to the tree!

In this case, our tree is our relationship with Jesus Christ. We cannot be focused on the fruit, but we must be attending to our relationship; and as a result, fruit will be produced without a conscious effort! You have to *abide* in Christ, which means to make your home in him. You have to find your life, your comfort, and your peace in Christ alone.

God, I want to abide in you. Help me to carve out my love, security, and comfort in you and you alone. I want to be more patient and more loving, but I realize that the only way to pursue these things is to pursue you. Offer me guidance and direction as I read your Word and learn what it means to surrender all to you. I praise you in advance for the mighty work that you are going to do in my heart as I am transformed by your love.

Jn 5 No branch can bear fruit by itself; it must remain in the vine. Neither can you bear fruit unless you remain in me. I am the vine, you are the branches. If you remain in me and I in you you will bear much fruit! apart from me you can do nothing. If you obey my

commands, you will remain in my love. I have told you this so that you

Idols | Exodus 20:1-17

When you step into the runner's role, you commit to giving time, energy, and resources to the cause of running. It is not long before your life is consumed with your schedule that operates around your running plans and when you don't get a run in for the day, you are left feeling unsatisfied.

You begin to serve running, and rather than it being an addition to your life it becomes the essence.

When thinking of idols we often rewind to the Old Testament golden calf and Asherah poles, but in reality, we boast in many idols today. An idol is simply an object of extreme devotion.[1]

J.D. Greear in his book *Gospel* describes the way in which you can identify idols in your life. Greear writes, "When something becomes so important to you that it drives your behavior and commands your emotions, you are worshipping it."[2]

Review these tough questions for a potentially tough revelation:

1. What is one thing you most hope is in your future?
2. What is one thing you most worry about losing?
3. If you could change one thing about yourself, what would it be?
4. What thing have you sacrificed most for?
5. When do you feel most significant?
6. What triggers depression in you?
7. Where do you turn for comfort when things are not going well?

I realized that running was an idol in my life after looking at these questions. I worried about losing my fitness to injury, I sacrificed so much time and energy, and I felt most significant when I ran well.

How about you? What else seems to be the master of your life? It is important to realize that idols are not always bad things—we make good things bad things when they turn into God things.

Repentance is the first step in reevaluating your walk and bringing it to a place that is built on stable ground. Change your mind and heart to see that God has more for you.

Reflect:

"Those who cling to worthless idols
turn away from God's love for them" (Jonah 2:8).

"I will destroy your idols and your sacred stones from among you; you will no longer bow down to the work of your hands" (Micah 5:13).

"Seek ye first the
Kingdom of God,
and all these things
shall be added
unto you."

Victory | 1 Corinthians 15:54-58

As you step on the course, you are longing for victory. Victory looks different for every person. Maybe for you victory means actually winning the race, setting a personal best, beating last year's time, or simply completing the race to the best of your ability. We view victory or the fulfillment of our goal as a form of deliverance—as if it was an answered prayer or a way in which we now feel satisfied and complete. While this earthly victory brings you bits of satisfaction, it will never grant you full contentment. This victory is only temporary and it will soon fade.

Your victory—your deliverance—is found in Christ alone. Because Jesus came, died on the cross, and then rose again, we have victory over death and abundant life. There is no fear in death for our Savior has conquered it. He paid the price for creation's sin. He took every bit of the wrath that we deserve and praise the Lord that we can find victory in him.

God, thank you for deliverance out of the ways of the world, out of the dominion of darkness and into your light. I recognize that nothing I do or how fast I run changes the victory that I have in you. You have already run the race and finished perfectly. Thank you for sharing this gift for there is no reason you had to, but you simply love us unconditionally.

Transform | Luke 11:37-41

Everyone knows how to run a 4-minute mile. You need to run four 60-second quarters. Not a second more. But just because you know how to do it, doesn't mean that you can do.

What is your goal? Do you know what you would need to do to achieve that goal? Run certain splits? Run with a certain strategy? We all can envision the fulfillment of our goals and what it would take to get there. We have the information.

There are plenty of individuals who know so much about the Bible, but just because they know all the information on "how to be saved" does not mean that a transformation in their hearts has occurred. Just as a runner might know how to run a certain race, it does not mean that they have the heart to do it. It takes dedication or discipline to achieve their goal and transform it into a reality.

The bridge between information and transformation is experience. Not anyone can go out and run a four-minute mile; it takes years and years of training as you build a foundation. Sure, the first step is knowing how to do it but you will never get there if you don't act on it. The same is true in someone's spiritual walk (or run).

Sometimes we get caught in the rut of knowing the information, but not acting on it. We would rather live in sin than experience God's love, change our ways, and have our hearts transformed. A relationship with Jesus Christ and the experiences of his saving grace will bridge the gap between your information and a life-long transformation.

Oh God, I want to be transformed by way of experiencing you. You are all around, and I am ready to open my heart and mind to your everlasting presence. I pray that you would put opportunities in my path that I might encounter you. Give me the wisdom and courage to pursue these opportunities as I learn from you and lean on you.

Time Out | 2 Corinthians 4:16-18

How do you spend your time? Does it ever feel like you don't have enough time in the day to get it all done? We always seem to have time (or make time) to run or get in the extra workout when necessary. We sacrifice sleep and/or quality time with friends and family in the name of a race or workout.

Where do you spend the majority of your time? What are your priorities? *Stop. Think.*

Are early morning runs taking priority over daily quiet time? Why is it easy to make time for running and so hard to pray and read the Bible daily? *Now, really think.*

Why is it so hard to make time for Jesus who holds eternal bearings, but it is so easy to make sure we have spent an hour working in our exercise plan?

We are fleshly beings. We seek the temporary and often neglect the importance of the eternal. It is easier to see the tangible benefits of working out and it is so much harder to grasp the unseen kingdom that holds joy and wonder beyond our wildest imagination.

We must train our minds to sit still, but we cannot sit waiting for the desire to spend time with God to be instilled in us. We must make God a priority and through this, we will see the difference in our lives. Your thirst for him in your life will grow and you will find yourself making time for the Lord, because he alone is your King.

God, why is timing such a challenge? I have plenty of time in my day—I just need to make better use of it. Help me, Lord, to take time for you even if that means just sacrificing time on the Internet. It is easy for me to say, but it is so much harder to do. But I can do all things with your strength and wisdom. Show me the benefits of spending time with you and grow my heart into one that hungers and thirsts for your Word daily.

Form | 2 Corinthians 12:9-10

When you get tired in a race, your form is one of the first things that breaks down. Perhaps you clench your fists, tighten up your shoulders or drop your head. When you drop your eyes you lose focus on what is ahead of you and where you should be going. While you are still moving in the right direction, it becomes more difficult to push onward.

When times get tough, our worldly nature pulls our focus off of God. We get tired, begin to struggle, and we lose sight of the end goal. We often get caught up in ourselves. We are still moving forward, but we lose perspective and get wrapped up in the minor details. Trouble is ahead when we take our eyes off of the only thing that can really grant us complete satisfaction in life: a relationship with Jesus Christ.

Reflect:

What is wearing you down or stressing you out? By identifying what consumes your thoughts, you can learn how to refocus. When you take your eyes off of yourself and offer your thoughts and trouble in a heart of surrender, the Lord carries your burdens and calms an anxious heart (1Pet. 5:7).

Refocus and you will be surprised by the peace that can relax any clenched fist and anxious spirit.

Progress | 1 John 1:5-2:2

Is there a perfect way to run a race? Perhaps.

Have you mastered the perfect race strategy?

This perfect strategy may give you an ideal to work for or the perfect time may give you a goal, but "perfect" always seems to be distant. There is always more to be done and this can get exhausting as you strive for complete satisfaction.

Instead, we should be focusing on the progress rather than perfection. You should still be doing the best you can do, reaching for your "perfection" but not destroyed when it reveals itself to be unachievable.

In the same way, our faith in Jesus Christ does not have to be based on perfection, but we can rejoice in the progress. Fortunate for us, Jesus was perfect and covered all of our imperfection so that beating ourselves up over it is no longer an issue. We can live in the freedom of working and living to the best of our abilities without fear of condemnation (Rom. 8:1).

Let us rejoice in progress: practicing self-discipline, learning to hear God's voice, repenting, and living in God's grace, love and mercy.

Dear Lord, wow. I thank you for not having to be perfect, because you know that is impossible. I praise you that you have already taken care of that in light of your Son's sacrifice. Let me not become lazy in my journey with you—help me to actively seek you every step of the way. Allow me to rejoice in the progress of conforming to the image of your Son rather than living in the guilt of falling short. Keep my eyes focused on what is ahead, forgetting what is behind so I can more fully see you.

Process | Matthew 6:14-15

Have you been through the "getting back in shape" process? There are days that are not filled with much hope for improvement accompanied by days of small breakthroughs and successes. You wish you could snap back overnight, but are reminded of the realities of the slow process and the hard work that comes along with it.

Forgiveness follows a similar path. It is a process. Whether you are forgiving someone else or yourself, you expect it to happen quickly or in moments of remorse. Wouldn't that be nice?

We need to compare forgiveness to getting back in shape. It is a daily workout. The best part of forgiveness is that you do not do it by yourself. God speaks life into your soul as you encounter the hard days or people in your life that hold a hard spot in your heart. God knows what it means to forgive as he has offered the ultimate sacrifice and forgiven us. Let us conform to his image.

Practice positive self talk like you would in your training, fixing your heart and mind on the end goal. Surrender this process to God and let him be your personal coach offering abounding comfort and peace.

There is hope in the process if we don't give up, but keep working through.

My Holy and Perfect God, free me and bring me into your forgiveness so I can freely forgive others. The first step of forgiveness is repentance—this is my call of repentance. I am ready to turn away and pursue you, not the bitterness that once consumed me. Before I served bitterness, but now I only want to serve you. Bitterness is exhausting, while you are life giving. Remind me daily that when your Son died on the cross he did not just die to forgive my sins, but to forgive the sins that were done against me. I rejoice in the freedom that you give me. Open my heart to accept it, God!

Daily Training Thought: Surrender

Our minds are a battlefield in which a realm of spirituality is encountered. We have to consciously choose to give up the wills of the flesh and submit to the will of the Spirit.

Before you run or compete, try this activity that symbolizes the physical surrender you are trying to wrap your mind around. If we force our bodies into submission of our will (and ultimately the Lord's will), our minds will accept the circumstances just like when we are competing.

Find a time and space to be alone. Close your eyes and reach your hands up to the sky. Reach to the heavens and breath deeply a number of times. Feel a physical burden lifted from your body. Bring yourself into the presence of the Lord and ask him to renew your mind, soul, and body. Surrender it all.

You can make this a daily practice. When you get up in the morning, surrender your day to the Lord. Cast your cares upon him (1 Pet. 5:7) and submit to the Lord (Jas. 4:7).

Reflect:

"...and call on me in the day of trouble; I will deliver you, and you will honor me" (Psalm 50:15).

Talent | Matthew 25:14-3

We have all been given various abilities in light of our running. Some are simply blessed with a greater talent, while others work just as hard to only be half as good. The actual talent or ability should not be the focus, but the ability to make the most of your talent is the important piece.

Reflect on the Parable of the Talents told by Jesus.

Each man was given a bag of gold according to his ability. We have each been given a talent according to our ability. After the master leaves, the servants are to make the most of their gold according to what they have been given. When the master returns, each servant must present what was made of his gold. Notice that the first two servants were given different amounts of gold, but because they made the most of what they had, the master replied with equal encouragement: "Well done, good and faithful servant" (v. 21-23).

But the third servant buried his gold in the ground and made nothing of it. The servant says, "I was afraid." In response, the master takes away the one bag of gold that was given to him and then scorns the servant for making nothing of his talents.

In both our running and daily lives, God has given us various talents and abilities to use for his glory—multiplying the potential of what we have been given. God does not want us to squelch what he has given us. We are to work our hardest for his glory and make the most of all that we have been given. Do not live in fear of failure, but work out your gifts.

God, thank you first of all for my talents. Help me to make the most of my talents so you will be glorified. I do not want to fear the outcome of failure of dissatisfaction like the third servant, but I want to continue learning what it means to serve you with my whole heart—no reservations.

Plan | 1 Samuel 15:22-23

Have you trained for a race and used a training plan to guide you along the way? It helps immensely to have some guidance and accountability within your practice to stay on track. While the plan is helpful, it is easy to lose sight of your overall goal or purpose as you begin living by the plan. When you begin serving the plan rather than your purpose, you risk getting tired and burnt-out. Or when an injury emerges, you forget your overall purpose and continue to serve the plan despite your common sense rulings to take a break. Keep your goals in sight and challenge yourself within the plan.

Can you relate this to the Christian walk in which you begin serving a plan rather than your purpose? You get up, go to church, maybe try to read your Bible and pray, but it is all just going through the motions? You begin to lose sight of your joy and overall goal that you are pursuing. Plans can be so helpful, but when you lose the heart's intent behind them, you run the risk for burnt-out and potential injury.

It is not all about the law or the rituals, but the obedience of the heart behind the actions. Continuously remind yourself of your purpose and motivate yourself by remembering the blessings that are constantly showered upon you.

Daily devotionals and guides for Scripture reading are very helpful. I encourage you to find one that speaks to you and dig into the Scripture to grow and learn as a child of God, but do not get caught up in serving the plan rather than serving your purpose.

God, thank you for creating me with purpose. I realize that my purpose above all else is to love you and love others. Show me how to live in love and pursue your truth daily. Discipline is difficult, but help me to refocus my sights on your kingdom for that is where the treasure lies.

Controllables | Matthew 5:1-12

Do you ever become overwhelmed by the "what if" factors that you might run into on race day? Do these looming thoughts ever bleed over into your enjoyment, love and freedom to run? And sometimes we are too busy trying to analyze the "uncontrollables" rather than embracing what we *are* in control over.

Uncontrollables could be other competitors, the weather, your body (or stomach) just isn't feeling it. There are things we can control such as our own peace of mind and our confidence in training. Beyond that, it is time to run and see what happens. There is no use in getting stuck on the things you have no control over, because you drive yourself into madness.

Jesus gave us a framework for living, not a play by play of how to do it. We should be holding on to the life lessons that he gave us instead of trying so hard to interpret the grey area. If the grey area was of the utmost importance, he would have defined it. We often get stuck on the grey that holds little significance in the scheme of the gospel; therefore, we lose sight of the controllable factors.

We don't know every bit of what is right and wrong, black and white; so let's live life through the lens that we know is the absolute truth: love the Lord your God with all your heart, soul and mind and love your neighbor as yourself. Seek first his kingdom and all else will be added to you (Matt. 6:33).

God, as I race and run for your glory give me peace in competition to give all that I have—not submitting to the anxiety and fear of the race. Your Word has given me a framework for life and I want to honor that. Lord, please guide me in the message of your Son that I may be more like him. I trust that the rest of the details will unveil themselves in your holy and perfect timing. I will continue to seek your kingdom.

Listen | Revelation 3:19-22

Have you ever run a race and had someone come up to you afterwards and say, "Could you hear me cheering for you?!" There have been times in which I bashfully answer, "No, I'm in the zone. I could not hear anyone really."

There are other times you can really hear people cheering for you or you can hear one person in particular. The only way you can ensure that you will hear someone's cheer is to specifically and intentionally listen for their call. For example, I am always listening for my mom's whistle or the advice of my coach as I come around each turn. But unless I am intentionally listening to the fans, the voices blur into a mass of noise.

Many people believe that God has never spoken to them. But is it that God has never spoken or that their ears are not listening and attentive to what God has to say? We will hear God only when we open our ears and our hearts. You cannot pass through your days not listening and not looking for God, but then be frustrated when you don't hear from him. You must be expecting him to reveal himself to you at any moment.

Pray that God would reveal himself to you throughout your day and when he does that you would have a willing heart to accept his will and his call. Tune into the Lord—his voice is more encouraging than any cheerleader on the sideline.

My Holy Counselor, I am ready to hear your voice. Open my ears, my heart and my mind, to listen to the will you want me to pursue for my life. Your call may not be loud, but Lord, that will not stop me from seeking you. Speak to the depths of my heart and allow me to be receptive to whatever you have for me. All the while, I will continue to walk in your ways as I love you and your people.

Terms | Proverbs 1:1-7

Have you ever experienced a true runners' conversation? It is as if runners have constructed their own language. Everyone throws out times, distances, and weird words; before you know it, the average person is extremely lost and confused.

How familiar are you with this running language? PR, fartlek, threshold, intervals, chip time, DNF, negative splits, strides, VO2 max, lactic acid, pace.

When you are familiar with this "running language," you simply feel more knowledgeable as you are capable of carrying on a good conversation with a group of runners.

I know I have some friends that when you start talking track times it sounds more like "I went a 72 on the 538 for a 2:22 and finished with a 7:34" rather than actual conversation.

How often do you feel lost in "Bible Talk" while you are in church, a conversation, or trying to read the Bible on your own? It may seem like gibberish, but do not be discouraged! This is how runner talk once was for you (or maybe you are still working on it). It takes time and an attitude apt for learning.

Open your heart and your mind to be taught and learn.

"Bible talk" was never something that Jesus was an advocate for. Rather, he wanted the message of the gospel to be one for all people. You are "all people" and Jesus is ready to speak to your heart openly and honestly without the exact knowledge of "terminology."

God, I pray that you would open my eyes to your Word and open my heart and mind to understanding it. I ask for the discipline and the endurance to continue reading the Bible and seeking you. Who you are and your will is revealed to me in this book, so allow me to take hold of all that you have for me by reading, learning and growing in you.

Simplicity | Matthew 22:34-40

In a race, the goal is simple:

Run as fast as you can from start to finish.

There are a plethora of helpful tools, but without this main idea, everything else is pointless.

We can follow the commands of the Bible, but if we don't have the core message of God's Word…everything else is pointless.
As Jesus' followers, we must proclaim that Jesus is Lord.

Jesus came to earth as fully man and fully God to dwell among us, teach us about his kingdom, die on a cross paying the ultimate price for our sin, AND he rose again conquering both sin and death.

The early church multiplied by the thousands because the message was simple. Today, we often get lost in the complexity.

Know the message and build everything else upon that.
Train hard, eat well, race smart. (So we can run fast.)
Love God, love others, make disciples. (Because we know Jesus is King.)

Oh, God, forgive us for the mess we have made of your Son's message and guide us in redeeming your original instruction to love you and love others. I know I get mixed up in the details when I should throw it off and run the race you have laid out for me. Help me fix my eyes on you, running towards you, and remembering your greatest commandment along with your sacrifice.

Temple | 1 Corinthians 6:12-20

Your body is your vehicle to movement. It is the means in which you can live, create and be you. As runners we understand the importance of our bodies, because without them we would lose a piece of who we are.

We cannot believe that just because we are runners that we are healthy. Be attentive to your exercise, your diet, and your holistic lifestyle that you are living. We are called to live a life full of health in the name of the Lord.

In 1 Corinthians, Paul tells us that our *bodies* were bought at a price with the blood of his Son; therefore it is our responsibility to be the caretaker of these precious prizes.

We are to take care of our bodies not only because God created them, but because God created them as a temple of the Holy Spirit. While the temple is a dwelling place of God, the actual temple in Jerusalem was also a place of sacrifice. And since our bodies have become the temple, God has met the required sacrifice in Jesus Christ.

Not only have our bodies been given to us as our responsibility, we have been given the responsibility to share what God has done in our lives.

Read and reflect on 2 Chronicles 7:1-3. Do you see the Old Testament parallels of the presence of God in the Solomon's temple to our temples now?

Power | Luke 10:17-20

Jesus has given you power. A special gift. The ability to run.

Or maybe you have been given multiple gifts like being good at your job, relating to others, making people laugh or [you name it].

It is first important to recognize that this ability to do what you do is of God and from God.

But let's take one more step back.

After Jesus sends out the 72 followers in Luke 10, they speak of their success in driving out demons and rejoicing in the ability that has been given to them. Jesus says, "Hold up" though. They shouldn't be rejoicing in this power he has given them, but the work that the Father has already done for them (and will continue to do in them).

You have been given the power to move mountains for the kingdom of God, but do not rejoice in this power—rejoice in the power of the sacrifice of Jesus Christ that says I will love you no matter what. Nothing can separate you from his love (Rom. 8:37-39).

God, thank you for your Spirit and your power that has been given to me to do good work in the name of your kingdom. You have given me the responsibility to represent you and I want to do that to the best of the abilities that you have given me. And Lord, you tell us that those who believe, they will do even greater things than the works of your Son (John 14:17). I am ready and willing to be transformed into your vessel of love and life change.

Persistence | Luke 18:1-6

Repeats are a central workout for the runner as you work on pace and mental toughness, preparing yourself for race day. And not only do you repeat distances in workouts, you repeat your training every day. You run miles and miles in order to produce results. You have an idea of your final goal, and you do whatever you can to reach that point.

You are practicing persistence.

In Luke 18, we meet the persistent widow who pled with the judge every day for justice. Finally the judge granted her justice because of her persistence in asking. She knew what she needed and did not give up until that goal was reached. Jesus told this parable to give an example about the importance of praying persistently and not giving up. Your running repetition brings results just as your prayers can. Your prayers can make a difference when you are asking in accordance with the Lord's will. You know his will by getting to know him as it is laid out in Scripture.

Reflect and rejoice in these passages:

"And this is the confidence that we have toward him, that if we ask anything according to his will he hears us. And if we know that he hears us in whatever we ask, we know that we have the requests that we have asked of him" (1 John 5:14-15).

"Have faith in God," Jesus answered. "Truly I tell you, if anyone says to this mountain, 'Go, throw yourself into the sea,' and does not doubt in their heart but believes that what they say will happen, it will be done for them. Therefore I tell you, whatever you ask for in prayer, believe that you have received it, and it will be yours. And when you stand praying, if you hold anything against anyone, forgive them, so that your Father in heaven may forgive you your sins" (Mark 11:22-25).

Insanity | 2 Corinthians 5:11-15

Runners are often called crazy. Have you been called crazy for your early mornings, late nights, long runs, cold runs, hot workouts and everything in between?

While some call it out of our mind, we prefer to call it dedication. It makes sense for us though. There is a goal that we are striving for and we are willing to make sacrifices and perhaps appear crazy to others.

In fact, do you ever enjoy the "You're crazy!" as you spit out the "eh, I just ran eight (miles) today"? We understand what Paul is saying in 2 Corinthians. Paul was told he was out of his mind for his preaching of the gospel, but he knew he had a goal. He had an experience with God himself that compelled his Spirit to do nothing else but share his love for Christ. Paul probably got used to being called crazy and thrived in the greatness of his mission.

He might have appeared crazy to others, but Paul understood his purpose and pursued it with his whole being. Are you willing to put in a little crazy dedication for the Savior of the world?

Reflect: What are you willing to sacrifice for your relationship with Christ? Are you ready to surrender your ways that seem good for God's ways that will bring you eternal hope? Ask God to fill you with a hunger for his presence and an understanding that gives you hope and peace.

Opportunity | Ephesians 5:15-17

On race day, there is always the opportunity to push harder and go faster. During your race you have a choice to make each second: go faster, maintain pace or slow down.

Anyone that has come within seconds of a goal or a record wonders if they could have dug *that* much deeper for another second. And anyone that knows that they have left everything on the course—knowing they could have done nothing more—are satisfied.

As Jesus' disciples we are in the same position each and every day. We can continue to work harder, reach more and live fuller, or we can live comfortably while we maintain or regress. We must be the people that leave everything on the course—knowing we did everything we could have done in order to reach our goal.

We must be the type of people who look and act upon every opportunity that God puts before us.

In the end, if we are living fiercely for Christ, we will be much more satisfied than if we just missed our goal by a few steps or seconds.

How can you be making the most of every opportunity that you are presented with? It takes a mind that is constantly asking, "God, what will you have me do today?"

"His master replied, 'Well done, good and faithful servant! You have been faithful with a few things; I will put you in charge of many things. Come and share your master's happiness!' (Matthew 25:23)

Pain | Mark 14:32-42

In the heat of the race when everything is telling you to give in besides your will, would you categorize that as "sprinkled with suffering" or "immersed in agony"? If you are doing it right, you should be immersed. There is pain, but in the pain there is great reward. You are aware of the victory that will result from the agony if you only hold on until the time is right.

Jesus understands the concept of agony in return for reward.

The price of sin is death and while we deserved death, he sacrificed himself by the will of the Father in the most painful torture and humiliating death of the Roman Empire. It was excruciating. But as his fate was laid before him, he prayed, "Father, your will be done" (v. 36). God unleashed his wrath on his only Son that he might have victory; thus we might have victory.

Now we are to run the race, while Jesus carries the burden of the pain so we can embrace the journey. It is difficult to look outside of your own needs when you are dying on a run or in a race. And it is much easier to be a light to others when you are not in deep agony. Jesus has taken our load so we can help those who are struggling around us.

You understand pain in a unique way. Praise God for victory amidst agony and the ability to live life in freedom.

Mighty King, thank you for pain. While it isn't pleasant, it reminds me of how little control I have of this world and all the control that you have. I praise you for the steadfast perseverance that you offer me in my weakness that allows me to overcome struggles. Again, all of this is because of you, nothing that I have done. I could do nothing apart from you. Sure, I could do things that don't hold any significance in the will of eternity. But with you, God, I can make a difference in my life and in the lives of the people I encounter every day.

Lessons from the Stumbling Series

My senior year of high school I asked God for humility and by the end of that year, I found myself flat on my face. I was humbled.

What began as an unprecedented, PR breaking cross country season, slowly declined into something out of my control. By the last three races of my final year, my body began shutting down just one or two miles into the race before I was lost in a haze and unable to maintain pace. I kept pushing, thinking I was stuck in a mental block of some sort. The last race of the season at the state finals, I was on pace for a personal best until the last 15 meters. I started slowing and eventually tumbling to the ground. I lost control of my body and any effort to move forward made me look even more helpless. I don't remember much besides going to the ground on my knees and somehow stabilizing to walk/crawl to the finish line. I made it across and was attended to by a group of people who managed to bring me out of the "haze" some time later.

I was embarrassed to have my last high school season end this way. I was trained and ready for anything, but something out of my control disconnected. I hid behind this moment in feelings of shame and embarrassment (none of these thoughts being the word of God). It was not until much later that I realized all the good that God had in store for me: a new sense of humility and ability to surrender.

Our enemy, Satan, often takes our situations that seem hopeless and presses us down so we feel angry and ashamed. This is all a front in order to distract us from the good that God is reconciling in our lives. Satan spews regret, while God speaks grace. Satan beats up, while God gives life. Satan says do, while God says *done*.

Perfect Conditions | Ecclesiastes 11:4

Weather is a huge factor in the training plan. For some it will make or break the outcome of a race or workout. Will it be too cold, too hot, too rainy? If you waited for perfect running conditions every day, you would not get out to run very often.

You have to embrace the rainy days, the chilly days, and the hot days. If you want to become a better runner, you have to prepare for the adversity and diversity of the days.

On the other hand, there are some scenarios in which going out and running would be plain dumb. For example, it is smart to steer clear from raging hurricanes, roads covered with black ice, or tornadoes falling from the sky. We all know that running in conditions like those would have little to no positive pay off.

In the same way, you must evaluate your risks when it comes to reaching someone for Christ. If you wait for the perfect conditions to step out in faith, nothing will happen. Just like you judge the weather, you must size up your risks and opportunities for outreach. When the Spirit speaks, are you ready to move?

When a decision is impulsive and not God-breathed, you might as well go for a long run when it is 110 degrees outside. As followers of Christ, we must take the right risks and pursue opportunities for furthering the kingdom.

While it might be uncomfortable as you slosh through the mud in a race, you know it is making you better and you will produce results. While it might be uncomfortable to go out of your way just to ask someone how he or she is doing, you know you are being the light of Christ.

Seek opportunities for outreach and ask those around you how you can be serving them.

Infusion | Jeremiah 23:23-24

Running requires whole mind, whole body, and whole life dedication for optimal results; running morphs into a lifestyle rather than a weekend hobby. All aspects of life impact how your running goes whether it be your emotions, energy levels, or even relationships. If you are a runner, it often means your lifestyle and schedule look somewhat different than someone who does not run.

All bits of our lives impact our relationship with the Creator in the same way each part of our lives affect our running. Our emotions, diets, routines, hobbies, jobs, dreams and passions all filter into the scheme of our existence which is entirely spiritual.

Spirituality should not be reserved for a compartment in your life, but it should be the essence of your life. We were not called to separate our faith from every other part of our lives, because our faith is what gives us life.

Our culture has separated secular and sacred, saying there cannot be an infusion. But if we are to live with Jesus as our example, we are going to see God in everything. When we see God in everything, it is impossible to separate God from any part of his creation and any part of our lives. To be a spiritual runner, it is not a matter of separating from the secular, but embracing the Spirit and presence of God wherever and whenever.

God, I realize that I dedicate my whole body and my whole mind to running. Take my passions for running, Lord, and mold them into passions to serve and love you with my whole body and whole mind. Forgive me for making running the essence of my life when you gave it to me to glorify your kingship. Redirect me in ways that I can worship through my running. Take every part of my life and use it for your glory. It is time to quit compartmentalizing. I give all for one, as you have given your one for all.

Relationships | 1 Corinthians 15:33-34

What causes so much pain, but also so much pleasure? Running. It is quite the love-hate relationship.

Nerves before a race can weigh you down. Some days your body is dragging. You are not able to reach your goal time. You think to yourself, "Why do I put myself through so much pain!? So much suffering!?" But then one great run happens. You find yourself in a state of pleasure as all the pain becomes worth it.

What about relationships? I will ask the question again: What causes so much pain, but also so much pleasure?

Conflicts between friends, family members, co-workers, and random acquaintances are inevitable. Chances are you have stressed, cried, or lost sleep over a relationship at some point in your life. But all the while, relationships bring us so much joy!

Family and friends are a beautiful gift. You create a multitude of life-long memories that cause you to forget about the pain that many relationships have brought you.

Build your relationships in and upon Christ because he is the sustainer. While there is always conflict, God will continuously redeem your relationships when they are built on the foundation of Christ.

Thank God for your relationships and remember to pray continuously for those who you impact and those who impact you.

Reflect:

"Walk with the wise and become wise, for
a companion of fools suffers harm" (Proverbs 13:20).

Cross Training | 1 Chronicles 16:23-31

Cross training improves the overall fitness and wellbeing of the runner. Not only does it offer a mental break from pounding the pavement, but it also works different muscles, making you stronger. Running is a forward movement, and we often neglect our lateral muscles causing injury.

We should be well-rounded athletes who lift weights, strengthen the core, and can bear to bike a hard workout. By working different muscles and strengthening your entire body, you become a better runner. You also feel more confident in your training, knowing that you are doing all that you can do.

Your relationship with Christ is not a one-way street, but a multi-faceted relationship of fellowship, scripture reading, prayer, singing, running, serving, and giving. You want to be strong and secure in your relationship, knowing that you are giving all you have. By only going to church on Sunday morning, you are missing out of the potential fullness of your life! By working different parts of your spiritual being, you can experience the strength and life behind the action.

If you have not already, begin to explore different spiritual exercises that expand your understanding of God and his will.

Try just five minutes of prayer and stillness. Ask someone what their favorite Bible verse is and dig into the origin of its writing. There are so many options—dare to explore.

Reflect:

"And whatever you do, whether in word or deed, do it all in the name of the Lord Jesus, giving thanks to God the Father through him" (Colossians 3:17).

Domino | Romans 5:1-8

I do not think there is a group of people that understand the meaningfulness of rejoicing in suffering better than runners. Who else willingly puts themselves through pain in order to become better, stronger people?

It seems the more pain you are willing to put yourself through in training, the greater chances there are for success and victory in competition.

We cannot disagree with this biblical domino effect from Romans 5: suffering produces perseverance, perseverance produces character, and character produces hope. We suffer to teach ourselves perseverance in which we build character and then we have hope for victory! Suffering ultimately prepares you for the future.

Have you ever been able to apply your past races, runs or workouts to future feats? These experiences fuel your fire and encourage you to persevere. The pain of the past has proved that it can push you through. You have new knowledge, a new strategy, or new motivation to draw from.

Take a look at your daily walk. Think of a difficult situation you have persevered through and how it has made you a better person and ultimately strengthened your faith. The Mighty Sculptor is constantly sculpting your character. With the deepening of your character, there are so many possibilities for hope in the future. You have been refined by your past sufferings and you are prepared for the path God has put ahead.

Even though we understand why we put ourselves through physical pain to be better athletes, we still find it hard to understand why we must endure suffering and hardship in our lives. Each struggle prepares you for eternal glory that calls for rejoicing!

God thank you for the pain that makes me stronger. While suffering is not enjoyable, it is in these moments that you teach what it means to surrender and follow you. Strengthen me, Lord, when the path is unsure for I know that your ways are higher than mine (Isa. 55:8-9). I praise you for giving us the ultimate example of suffering in your Son who conquered the grave. You paid the price so I wouldn't have to and for that, I am eternally grateful.

Reflect:

"The righteous person may have many troubles, but the LORD delivers him from them all" (Psalm 34:19).

"And the God of all grace, who called you to his eternal glory in Christ, after you have suffered a little while, will himself restore you and make you strong, firm and steadfast" (1 Peter 5:10).

Community | Acts 4:8-13

I don't know about you, but my experience in the running community has been fantastic; whether it is on a team with my cross country family or hitting the roads for the summer 5Ks with dudes that look like they haven't stopped running for years.

Do you have people you run with on a regular basis? Or maybe you have other runners from work or school that encourage you or check up on how you're doing?

A common bond unites you. You have one goal and that is to finish the race to the best of your abilities or achieve a certain goal. I always find the camaraderie among racers to be so comforting and fun! I hope you have experienced this at some point (if not, find yourself a positive crew to encourage you!).

The camaraderie of runners brings to life some foundational aspects of the early church. The believers of the early church were united by a single purpose as they proclaimed the gospel. They were bold, prayed together and encouraged one another. They were so moved by the weightiness of their message that they were willing to risk everything and put it all out on the line.

Reflect: How often do you find yourself putting everything out on the course or the track to reach your goal? Even if it means blood, sweat, and tears? What if we take the same runners' mentality of total sacrifice of our bodies to achieve a goal and transform it to the ministry of Jesus Christ? What if we are so moved by his life that we are willing to leave our pride aside to commit our lives to eternal glory for a goal that is so much greater than ourselves?

Appearance | 1 Samuel 16:1-7

You could say that someone has a "runner's body" or "looks like a runner," but that does not limit who the runner can be.

Sometimes the most unlikely people are incredible runners. It does not matter what they look like or sound like as much as it matters what they run like. Their running ability is measured in their ability to work hard and keep themselves motivated. We have an ideal "runner look" in mind, but there are no limits to appearance.

When Samuel went out looking for the next king of Israel, he had an ideal appearance in mind. He went to the house of Jesse as the Lord instructed him to do, but the king was not found in the most likely form. David, the youngest and smallest of Jesse's son was the one chosen by God as the next king of Israel.

God chooses to look at the heart rather than the outward appearance. What a cool lesson in the character of our God that it does not matter what we look like, smell like, sound like, how tall or how short, but he looks only at the heart.

This also affirms the message of Jesus Christ—the gospel is not reserved for one people group. Everyone has the opportunity to change the state of their hearts, not their appearance.

Praise him who takes us for our hearts rather than our looks!

God, thank you for choosing me as your child. While I am beautifully created in your image, I praise you for not judging me based on my appearance. Constantly remind me that I am not to judge anyone by their appearance. Let the lesson of David teach me that sometimes the most unlikely individuals are chosen for your biggest jobs for the kingdom. You made this clear in your Son, Jesus. Nothing pointed the people to your Son by the way of his looks but by the words of his heart.

New | 2 Corinthians 4:16

The morning after a high adrenaline race, workout, or run (good or bad) can be a mix of emotions.

A good day: you don't have a hard time replaying the glory of your experience. A bad day: you would rather roll over, and push looming thoughts away.

Regardless of the situation, it is your responsibility to get back out there. Another day ahead. Another day of training. Preparing for the next opportunity.

Daily, we have the same responsibility as followers of Christ. We cannot dwell on the past, but we can rejoice in the gift of a new day and ultimately new life. If you were to bask in the glory of a particular race and rely on pride rather than training, you are not giving your best in humility. If you allow yourself to be defined by a bad workout, you sink into a pit of apathy.

We don't have to be who we were yesterday or even be defined by the good things that we do or represent. We are seen through the eyes of a Creator God who uses Christ's perfection as a lens to see us. He makes all things new. Wake up today and feel refreshed to new opportunities.

God, help me shake off the past and pursue the new day that you have set before me. Each day has new challenges, defeats and victories, and I am encouraged by your love that tells me I can do all things through you. Refresh my heart and mind to seek you today.

Reflect:

"When anxiety was great within me, your consolation brought me joy" (Psalm 94:19).

Iron | Proverbs 27:17

An inevitable truth: when you train with someone who is better, faster, and stronger than you, you are bound to improve. You are pushing yourself to keep up with their pace and working hard so easy runs can actually be easy. If you consistently train with someone who is a faster runner than you, you will see the difference in your performance.

When you surround yourself with people who build you up, challenge you in discussions, suggestions and ideas, and strive to lead Christ-centered lives, you will see this reflected in your daily walk. Just as iron is sharpened by iron when it is rubbed against another piece of iron, so is one person sharpened by another.

But imagine rubbing a piece of iron against a stick of butter. It would destroy it! There is nothing constructive that goes on by rubbing a piece of iron and a stick of butter together (except that you cut up the butter!).

In the same way, there is little sharpening that occurs by spending all your time with someone who is consumed by the ways of the world (Prov. 22:24-25). This should not be confused with an instruction not to hang out with those who do not follow Christ, but it is essential to find others that you may grow with, build one another up, and act as partners of love and accountability.

Lord, I praise you for bringing me to the place I am now—a springboard into a place of knowledge and growth as I actively seek you and all your Word has to offer me. Help me to refine the ways in which I live and be honest with myself as I interact with my friends and family. Surround me with people who are going to sharpen me so I may grow stronger in you.

7 Days Without Training Makes One Weak | Mark 14:32-42

You have decided to enter into a training plan to be the best runner that you can be and you have to make a choice:

1. Train for one hour per week or
2. Train multiple times throughout the week

Which one would you choose?

I hope you would choose the entire week for your training opportunities. You couldn't become a better runner by training once a week for an hour. There would be little focus and little improvement.

Why do we think we can become stronger in our faith by once a week encounters with the Lord or perhaps not seeking him at all? We would call someone foolish if they wanted to become a stronger runner by hardly training once a week; so why do we convince ourselves that we can be complete servants of Christ by only attending a church service on Sunday mornings?

If God was given a choice between spending one hour with you on Sunday mornings or the rest of your week, what would he choose? Seems like an easy choice.

God wants all of you, not just your Sunday Christian routine. He wants to see you grow and love Him more and more; this will not happen in one hour or once a week. It's time we seek God all week long for it is there that faithful strength is found.

Challenge: Build habits of prayer and reading the Bible one day at a time. Pick a verse this week and understand it. Google and research the verse if you have to! And then memorize it. This will keep your thoughts fixed on the Lord as you learn what it means to serve him with your life.

Foundational | Matthew 7:24-29

As a distance runner, you understand the importance of building a base. Weekly mileage becomes the foundation of your training as the miles add up and your endurance builds.

Without a foundation, runners who quickly bump up their mileage become more susceptible to injury. Distance runs not only build physical toughness, but also mental toughness. Your base gives you a place to work from and grow as a runner.

A strong foundation takes time, work, and help from others. This process looks different for everyone.

To build a foundation resistant to the winds and waters of this world, you must build yourself on the rock of Jesus Christ. Building this foundation is not easy and just like running, it takes time, work and help from others.

By building your relationship with Christ on solid rock, it does not mean that the storms of life will not come. It does mean that there will be something holding you up so you do not crumble into destruction.

Christ is the rock while all else is shifting sand.

Reflect: When you think of "rock," what do you think of?
Now imagine a huge rocky mountain. What comes to mind? If God is your rock and refuge, what does he offer? Think about this as you read Psalm 62:1-2.

Methodology | Psalm 139:14

What if all runners pursued the same training plan? How weird would that be? We know the same plan does not work for everyone (otherwise everyone would be doing it). There are various training programs based on preference that are equally effective depending on the runner.

While we are all created in God's image, we are all created uniquely. What if all people pursued the same means of worship? The same song, the same dance. There would be stiff conformity.

We don't all have to be doing the same thing for it to be the "right way" to worship. We are fearfully and wonderfully made, created to worship God fearfully, wonderfully and uniquely.

Just because we prefer different kinds of worship does not mean that one is more effective than the other.

Everything you do and everything that you are is an act of worship, it just is a matter of what you are worshiping. When you have your heart fixed on the Creator who made you to live for him, your life will be transformed into a great act of worship that is greater than you and fully focused on God.

God is holistic. He is shalom: the essence of wholeness, completeness, and peace. Let us praise him that we have the opportunity to embrace a piece of him in our lives.

God, thank you for creating me. Forgive me for grumbling about what is "wrong" with me when I should be praising you for all you have given me. I pray that you would guide me in the ways of your righteousness so I can seek how to best glorify you with my life and talents. Thank you for the diversity in the body of believers! This offers such an awesome picture of your kingdom and who you are.

Church | Romans 12:3-8

Runners build community, eat together, encourage one another, hurting together, and train tough. Within running clubs, groups and friends, there is a common bond and sense of camaraderie. Sometimes these groups resemble the early church more than our churches do now.

Many people are turned off from the "church," but the church is not the building or even the service. The church should be a moving, active, fruitful group of people. It is not a group that meets once a week in the same place at the same time.

It is a place of growth and encouragement from the people around you as you meet together united in the gospel.

The church body should be together in fellowship often, adapting to their surroundings, eating together, sharing together, and interacting with new people all the time like we do with our running friends.

The church is described as the body of Christ. You know that a body cannot stay still and remain sane! The body requires movement and if the body isn't moving, it gets out of shape. In the same way, if the church is not active, growing and seeking people of the community, it is going to become out of shape and ineffective.

The most important part of any church is the mission of the gospel— the good news of Jesus Christ that frees you from the bondage of sin and brings you into a relationship of infinite love.

Reflect:

You are a part of the body of Christ, does your life reflect it? What are your gifts? How can you be contributing to an active body whether it be your running group or church?

Grumble | Philippians 2:14-16

"I really don't want to get up early this morning."

"I can't possibly run a decent time in this weather."

"My legs feel terrible."

Insert your excuses, complaints and grumbles here:

_____.

Now get rid of them.

What a different world it would be if we all laid our complaints to the side. If you were to come across someone who refused to complain about situations in their life (no matter what the situation), you would realize that something is different. Strive to be that person that refuses to complain.

The best way to eradicate your complaining is to replace it with praise. God says that if we stop our grumbling, we will be established as true followers of Christ. "Then you will shine among them like the stars in the sky" (v. 15).

Lord, I cannot do this without you. It is my sinful nature to grumble and complain, but I have faith that you can rescue me from the prison of my mind. Please free me from the shackles of the flesh and unleash me into the majesty and mystery of your will. Today begins a new day of seeking you and conforming to your image!

Mountain Top | Luke 9:28-36

Running up a hill or mountain is difficult—mentally and physically—but it makes you strong. We train up inclines to build strength for other runs and other races. While it is challenging, making it to the top is so rewarding.

There is an air of accomplishment and satisfaction. And if you are lucky, you are rewarded with the beauty of an aerial view as well. Most of the time, the struggle and journey up the hill is worth the feeling of achievement.

God meets us all the time wherever we are at, but we have a unique opportunity to meet God on the mountain (or even on your local overpass). In the Bible, God consistently reveals himself on the mountaintop whether it's Moses at Sinai (Exodus 19), Elijah at Horeb (1 Kings 19), or Jesus and his mountaintop transfiguration (Luke 9:28-36). The temple in Jerusalem is also considered the Holy Mountain or Mt. Zion.

Rejoice in the struggle up the incline for there is beauty in the revelation at the top. We do not only understand the physical struggle of people like Moses, Elijah and Jesus, but we understand the idea of achieving a prize at the top.

Ask God to meet you on whatever mountain you are climbing up and praise him in the process.

Reflect: When do you feel like you are climbing up a mountain spiritually? Ask God to constantly refresh you on your journey, because he is with you every step of the way. Remember that when you reach the top, you always come back down. Don't live satisfied only when you reach relief at the top, but turn to the Lord and praise him always.

Freedom | Isaiah 40:29-31

Are you free? Free from fear of condemnation, the world, what others think of you, the future, your dreams and ambitions? If you are not entirely free, are you trusting God with your whole being?

Isaiah 40:31 is one of the more popular verses for runners as this scripture paints a picture that we really understand. We are dumbfounded to imagine what it would be like to run and not grow weary.

We are given three examples of the freedom we can experience if we surrender our hearts and trust God:

1. Soar high on wings like eagles
2. Run and not grow weary
3. Walk and not faint

The awesome part of this picture is that the author cannot fully capture the freedom granted by God even in these illustrations. God is so great and so beyond our comprehension.

He holds so many great promises for us if we secure our focus on him and trust. We must place our hope in him; not in our athletic talents, material objects, personal hopes, or dreams for the future.

God's promises are free and they are yours for the taking. You must set your focus on him, run for him, and you will renew your strength.

Challenge: Go through this day reminding yourself of the freedom you have in Christ and ask God to constantly teach you what it means to be his child.

What Really Matters | John 3:16-21

Scenario: I ran the mile, did back flips the whole time and finished in 5:15. Impressive, right?

You also ran the mile and finished the race in 5:14.

Who won? You did. Does it matter that I did back flips the whole time? No, I still lost.

While my back flips might have been impressive to the home crowd, the result sheet will only show the finishing times. In the same way, we don't need to be impressive with our works on earth to simply prove our goodness to other people. God sees us through the lens of his Son and his Son is perfection. There is nothing that we can do that makes him love us more and nothing we can do that makes him love us less. His love is truly unconditional.

This is only possible because of Jesus. And just as there is only one way to win a race (run the fastest time), there is only one way to God and that is through Jesus Christ. Jesus is "the way, the truth and life" and no one comes to the Father except through him (John 14:6). We serve him because we love him, not because we need him to love us.

When you love someone, your response is to serve. Our works should overflow out of our thankfulness. That is why faith *without* works is dead (Jas. 2:14-18); our lives should be a reflection of our grateful hearts. God cares about our hearts. Let us honor him with all of our lives.

God, you are a God of love. I praise you for the freedom of not having to earn your favor, and the joy of getting to serve you. You pour out your blessings on me while I am still so small and ungrateful. But Lord, thank you for making me your child and offering your Son as the way, the truth, and life. Teach me daily how I can grow more in you and serve you because I love you, not because I feel like I have to.

Origin | John 21:15-19

Workouts have a purpose. Specific exercises and diets all have a purpose. Sometimes I struggle to know what that purpose is though. I end up consulting my coach or searching the web and eventually the significance of the task is explained.

For example, why do I do strides after long runs? Muscle memory. Or why do I ever have to lift? Full body strength makes you a stronger runner as you drive up hills and work to maintain good form. While everything has a reason, it just takes some investigation.

If you haven't already, it's time to dig deeper into the origins of the Scriptures—especially when they don't make sense to us. The beauty of the Internet and a multitude of books is that we have Greek and Hebrew origins of words right at our fingertips. They all serve a certain purpose whether we realize it or not. It may just take a little bookwork and research to see what the author of the passage was *really* meaning. Use Google or reference BlueLetterBible.com for resources and commentaries.

For example:

There are three different types of love in the Greek language (*agape, phileo, eros*) of which two (*agape, phileo*) are used in the New Testament.

The first, *agape*, is used when referring a self-sacrificial love that is represented between God and Jesus and people should be exercising this sort of love to one another. (See John 15:13 and Ephesians 5:25.) There is also *phileo*, which translates into a manner of "brotherly love." Eros, on the other hand, means a sexual or erotic desire.

In John 21:15-16, Jesus asked Peter if he loved Him with the *agape* type of love and Peter responded that he had the normal human *phileo* type of love for Him. Later, after receiving the Holy Spirit, Peter would be able to genuinely demonstrate *agape* type godly love, serving others throughout his lifetime and making the ultimate sacrifice in martyrdom.[3]

God, help me to dig deeper into your Word so my relationship with you can grow. I ask that your Spirit would teach me and give me thirst to know more about you. Also, give me the gift of stillness as I sit down to spend time in your Word. Please, still my mind in the busyness of my days so that I can serve you fully.

Experience | Ephesians 1:17-23

People say we are crazy for running the way we do, but my first response is always: "You just have to try it for yourself." When you begin to set goals and achieve them, it starts a fire in your belly to push onward. The key to knowing the joys of running is experiencing it for yourself. You cannot begin to describe how great it feels to break your personal record to someone who has no idea what it feels like to run.

The beginning of a personal relationship with Jesus Christ begins in a similar manner: experience. Any relationship begins with experience. Think of your best friends—why are you such good friends? Often, you have experienced good and bad times together and have grown closer. God is waiting for you to experience his peace, love and goodness, but this can only happen if you choose to meet him.

So you may be saying, "I am ready to experience God, but how do I do that?" Pray for his revelation. The thing is that God is constantly revealing himself to us in all circumstances, but our eyes are not open to this realization. By praying for revelation, we are opening our eyes to see what God is and already has been doing in our lives.

When we begin to seek his revelation, we realize that we can experience a peace that transcends all understanding and a joy that lives above circumstances. God has gone the distance, we just have to open our hearts and meet him along the way.

God, I want to experience you. I am ready for you to open my eyes so I can encounter you daily. Reveal yourself to me so I can be filled with your love and your light. Thank you for meeting me where I am at and giving me your Word to teach and guide me.

Head Games | Proverbs 4:20-22

Have you become acquainted with the voice inside your head singing you praise or laments of defeat? It can be your best friend on a good day or your worst enemy on an off day. Practicing positive self-talk is essential to success. If you wake up the morning of your race telling yourself it is going to be ugly… well, it is going to be ugly.

You must fill your whole being with words of encouragement and positivity in order to get your mind right. Your mind becomes the engine.

"You are prepared. You are strong."

The voice inside your head is present not just on race day though. You live with it constantly and you dictate what is being spun through your head daily. By meditating on the Word of God and the wisdom and life it exudes, it will bring "health to one's whole body" (v. 22).

Bury your heart in the Word and you will find that your default state of mind is renewed. Instead of pity, there is strength. Negativity is replaced with thanksgiving. With the power of the Spirit, you have the ability to live above your circumstances and be encouraged by the conscience that once weighed you down.

Meditate on Philippians 1:9-11:

"And this I pray, that your love may abound still more and more in real knowledge and all discernment, so that you may approve the things that are excellent, in order to be sincere and blameless until the day of Christ; having been filled with the fruit of righteousness which comes through Jesus Christ, to the glory and praise of God."

Clothe Yourselves | Colossians 3:12-14

Have you ever been on a run and realized that you grabbed an uncomfortable pair or shorts or a shirt that fits weird?

Or worse yet… Have you ever put on a pair of shorts or shirt that you know is not comfortable, but you decide to be lazy and run in it anyway?

What we clothe ourselves with is so important. As runners, we make an effort to put on the best clothing in order to improve our performance in anyway we can.

Colossians 3:12 says we must clothe ourselves with compassion, kindness, humility, gentleness and patience. In the same way as the clothes we put on our physical bodies, we must make an effort to put on the best that we have in order to make our lives more like Christ's life.

Some days, we make a conscious effort to not care; we put on selfishness, pride, and greed, when we know it is not good for us. Eventually, we are convicted out of our self-righteousness.

So maybe it is easier to pick out the right things to wear, but what we carry with us in our hearts, attitudes and lives is what really matters in the long run.

Reflect: Pray and meditate on which of these five traits you could use more of. Ask God that you might abide in his love all the more that love, joy, peace, patience, kindness, goodness, faithfulness, gentleness and self-control will be the product of your life (Gal. 5:22-23).

Tune In | Acts 1:4-8

Are you one of those runners that prefers running with music in your ears? With headphones in your ears, you are focused on the music flowing through your head instead of your panting breath. If you were running without music at the same pace, you would be getting the same workout—but with the music, it doesn't seem as hard. The music seems to take a bit of your concentrated pain away as you are distracted by the tunes; the music also manages to pump you up.

This offers a beautiful picture of what life is like when you have accepted Jesus and live by the music of the Holy Spirit. The Spirit is your guide, counselor, comforter and advocate. You are no longer looking inward at your pain and panting breaths, but the consistency of God in your life. The circumstances and struggles in your life are not any less real, but you are able to take your eyes off of yourself and look towards your Heavenly Father that has all things under his rule and reign. His grace is sufficient and his joy fills you.

There is no magical reason that running is often easier with headphones besides you can't hear yourself huffing and puffing. In the same way, when we look beyond ourselves, we can rejoice in the beauty of the Holy Spirit's music.

God, you are mysterious and magnificent all together. Not only did you give your son to die on the cross so that I may have life, but you gave me your Spirit also. God, help me open my heart to you. Help me to look pass myself and seek you in all that I do. I praise you that I am able to have joy even when it's hard.

Greed | Luke 12:13-34

Is there another goal or another mark ahead always making you unsatisfied at the roots of your athletic performance? Are you getting stuck on what you have not achieved rather than what you have accomplished? If you are not in this position, do you know someone who is? There is a balance in wanting to do better and *never* being satisfied with an achievement. We balance this in an attitude of greed and gratitude when reflecting on our lives.

We understand the concept of "running greedy" to want more, do more, and be better, but when we begin to overlook the accomplishments bypassing all gratitude, it is time to refocus.

In our daily lives as followers of Christ, we cannot live in this same type of greed when it comes to our material possessions. Living like this only causes emptiness. It is possible to live in abundance while actually giving rather than getting. You become more full when you have served rather than shopped.

Our world today says consuming is healthy because it enhances the economy, while greed has spiraled out of control through consumerism. Jesus spoke to the scares of greed more than any other topical issue though. It is time to refocus our hearts on gratitude, thanking God for the abundance of what we have been given.

Reflect: Are you grateful for your ability to run or are you constantly unsatisfied and searching? What is your daily attitude? Grateful or discontent? Is greed something that impacts you? How can we change constant consuming into contentment?

Thirst | John 4:1-15

Physical thirst is a simple reminder of our human weakness. No matter how hydrated you are at one time or how much water you chug, it will never satisfy your thirst forever. God has created us this way so that in every instant we are left with thirst, we are reminded for our desperate need for him.

While he may be supplying you with drinking water, he also wants to give you his living water. He has offered us a drink that *will* satisfy. This satisfies our longing for purpose in life. Our worldly thirst will never be permanently quenched, but let this be our daily reminder of dependence.

God knows where you have been and the sin in your life, but all he sees is what his Son has done. Through his Son he has washed us white as snow (Isa. 1:18). God has an abundance of living water and while he is offering it to us, he is only waiting for our acceptance.

God, giver of this living water, I praise you for this gift of thirst which acts as a daily reminder of my need for you. You created us so perfectly and intentionally and thirst is a part of that. Help me use my weakness as a reminder of my need for you. I can do nothing apart from you, God (John 15:5).

Reflect:

"Come, all you who are thirsty, come to the waters; and you who have no money, come, buy and eat! Come, buy wine and milk without money and without cost" (Isaiah 55:1).

One | Ephesians 4:1-6

Have you been on the line at the start of a massive race? Or at least seen one? There are hundreds—if not thousands—of runners on the start line. They are all unique in their appearance and will all be unique in their race strategy, but they are all looking towards the same goal: the finish.

All these people lined up and ready to go. How often do we see a group of people that big all united in one cause? Just to finish the race.

This is an incredible reflection of the body of Christ. We are called to have "one Lord, one faith, one baptism" as we all move toward the same purpose. That does not mean that we are all the same people, but we have the same goals. We have different ways of getting there and all at different times, but we are moving as one.

Some run in pairs. Some struggle to keep their pace steady. Some simply do not have the power to finish this race with strength.

The race of life is not reserved for one person or one people group. *Anyone* can enter the race and everyone has the opportunity to finish.

God, thank you for the opportunity to start a new race each day surrounded by people of all backgrounds each with their own story. Although the kingdom is here, it is not yet fulfilled. Help me to seek this kingdom. Direct me to those who have the same passion for you as we serve one Lord under one faith in one baptism—we are the New Israel under your Son Jesus Christ.

Shadow | Psalm 121:1-8

When the sun is beating down, shade offers the ultimate relief. When you hit the shade on a blazing day, it is as if new life has come alive with you and you are energized for the next batch of sunshine. Recovering in the shade is a constant and ongoing process of breaking down and building back up.

"Because you are my help, I sing in the shadow of your wings" (Ps. 63:7).

The Lord is our shade and our shadow. Your shadow can never be far from you. It constantly follows you and is most visible when the sun is at its peak—shining down its heat.

"Each one will be like a shelter from the wind and a refuge from the storm, like streams of water in the desert and the shadow of a great rock in a thirsty land" (Isa. 32:2).

Jesus Christ is the ultimate shade. On the hottest days, he brings us in and offers us relief and protection from the rays and their heat. God always seeks the best interest of those who love him and while the heat can be draining, there is always joy to be found. Praise God for his protection from the heat and storms alike when we seek him (Matt. 7:24-29).

God, you are my mighty shade tree that cools me, refreshes me and strengthens me for the joys and trials before me. I pray that I seek your comfort before the comfort of anything or anyone else, because I know that you can sustain me. Forgive me for looking for refreshment in the wrong places—even in my running. You are the only one that can fuel me constantly and consistently.

Share | 2 Corinthians 1:3-7

Runners love to share running stories. Funny ones. Frightening ones. If anything, it makes for good conversation to pass the time on your long runs. We often take these stories from our past experiences and use them to help others as they prepare for their first races, new experiences or nervous ambitions.

We have a similar role in passing along the comfort of the Lord. If you have felt the comfort of the Lord, you have encouragement to share with others. God's great comfort is supposed to be given and received through his people. We are the hands and feet of Jesus Christ.

When speaking about comfort, Paul used the Greek word *paraklesis*. This is not interpreted as sweet hugging, but strengthening, helping or making strong as in preparation for the future. That is our role for those we encounter daily.

Find those who need prayer and encouragement; help them persevere through a struggle that you have encountered in your own life. Offer comfort from the Lord that transpires through you.

The result of the Corinthians' comfort produced a "patient endurance" for Paul. This Greek translation means, "steadfastness in the face of unpleasant circumstances."

We all desire patient endurance so be the light that supplies this hope and encouragement.

God, give me your eyes to see those who are hurting and need your comfort. I ask that you would guide me in my pursuit of comforting them so your life and love would shine through me. My pain is not easy to share, but I pray that it would be an encouragement to someone else who is struggling. You knit your kingdom together in mysterious, yet glorious ways and I praise you in advance for the way you will use me for your glory.

A Mind Full | Deuteronomy 6:4-9

Most runners have quite the ability to memorize personal records, splits from a race or specific times and distances. If you are not like this, I'm sure you know someone who is. I have teammates (and I'm guilty myself) who can rattle off 10 different obscure times from a race that was last week.

If you are not a running nerd, what do you find yourself able to memorize? Everyone takes to memorizing tons of information each day. We memorize information for school, work, movie quotes, and song lyrics. The things that are on our lips reflect our interests and personalities. We remember the things that are important to us.

If God is important to us, we need to have his Word on our lips and in our minds. Memory should not only be reserved for our mileage and workout splits. It is time to indulge in the Word for it is alive and sharper than any double-edged sword (Heb. 4:12). Find strength, scandal and inspiration there—it is relevant to your life and God is ready to speak his truth to you through it.

I challenge you to pick a verse and memorize it. Hang it on your walls, write it on your hands. Find an accountability partner and work together to keep this book of life we call the Bible on your heart, mind, and soul.

Don't forget: the Bible is still the world's #1 seller. Don't neglect God's precious gift to you.

Reflect:

"All Scripture is God-breathed and is useful for teaching, rebuking, correcting and training in righteousness…" (2 Timothy 3:16).

Balance | 1 Thessalonians 5:4-11

There are runs you do alone and others with a group. I think it is fair to say that both types of runs are helpful and it's nice to maintain a balance of each in your training.

There are days where a solo run with your thoughts or your iPod can put you in a needed place of meditation and peace. There are other days that you wouldn't dare get out without some accountability and encouragement from a friend or two.

Our worship takes a similar form.

Solo quiet time is essential for hearing the voice of the Lord in prayer, reading, journaling, moving, or stillness. Without these times it is easy to forget who you are in the midst of all that is scrambling around you. These times are good for being secure enough in yourself to be alone with God and your own thoughts.

Then there are other days that you need people. You absolutely need the encouragement and accountability from others—allowing yourself to be shaped and sharing your story to shape them.

You glean different but important things by being by yourself and being in a group. Don't neglect the balance. You can't be a solo Christian, but don't let your faith be defined by only those who are around you. Seek refuge in being fueled by the Spirit in all ways.

Challenge: Seek time to enjoy the company of others in discussion and fellowship, while also spending time alone with God. What does your balance look like now?

Prevention | Colossians 3:5-10

Half of training is injury prevention (or it should be at least). We check on the quality of our running shoes, stretch, ice, bike and swim when necessary. We have the ability to take care of ourselves so we don't get hurt. We can take precautionary measures so we don't end up injuring ourselves, damaging our bodies or our mental wellbeing. Injury prevention does not take up a lot of time or energy, but by doing the small things, it can make a huge difference.

Let's parallel our injuries to sin. What tempts you into separation from God? Lying, cheating, gossiping, over-eating, under-eating, pride, jealousy, [insert yours here]?

You have the ability to avoid injury by removing yourself from situations of temptation. If you have an issue with talking bad about other people, then perhaps it is time to spend less time with people who only talk negatively about others. You have the ability to take care of yourself so you don't get hurt! It takes some time and thought to be attentive to situations that cause you to stumble, but eventually you will be able to run in freedom without the fear of injury.

Just because you practice injury prevention does not mean that you will never get hurt; sometimes it is inevitable. But set yourself up for victoriously living by seeking your best interests under God's will for your life.

Dear Lord, your Son taught us how to pray as it is recorded in Matthew 6:9-13: "...And lead us not into temptation, but deliver us from the evil one." God, lead me not into temptation for in temptation there is a world of sin that I want nothing to do with. I am not a victim of sin, but a victor over sin because of your Son's life, death and resurrection. When there is temptation, I praise you because you always give me a way out (1 Cor. 10:13). Jesus offered us an example of this resistance as Satan tempted him—equip me to follow his lead so I may serve you with every piece of my life.

Response | Proverbs 15:1-18

In the middle of your race, your competitor comes up on your shoulder to pass. You have a choice to make. You can either let them pass or input a competitive surge. You can scrounge for any ounce of strength and pull from your hard work and training. How you respond to the circumstance determines the outcome of your race.

You may not be able to control what your competitor does next, but you have control over your response.

In every encounter with someone, you are given the opportunity to shine a light of joy. How many people do you know have been turned away from the Christian church because they have been hurt by the actions or response of another individual?

We are called to encourage one another and keep one another accountable in love. There should not be disunity in the body of believers because we are disrupting what we can control: a proper response.

Psalms and Proverbs are full of knowledge that tell us we are to show the love of God by being slow to anger and abounding in steadfast love. We are chosen to follow his response.

Read from Exodus 34:6, Numbers 14:18, and Psalm 103:8 to reflect more deeply on a proper response in light of the kingdom.

Discomfort | 1 Peter 4:12-19

If you aren't in some discomfort during your race, there is room for improvement (A.K.A. more discomfort). You are doing something right if you are in pain no matter how irrational that seems.

Jesus also calls us into a state of discomfort. I would not say that this is a constant state of discomfort, but one must possess the ability to handle prolonged circumstances of discomfort in the name of the Lord. Who else besides a pack of runners understands the principle of discomfort in order to achieve a victory that will last longer than the current pain?

Embrace discomfort and sacrifice in your walk with Christ. Seek opportunities to step out of your normal day to love, serve, and encourage others—looking beyond yourself and your own comfort.

God, you know all about discomfort as you watched your Son tortured on the cross. While we do not understand always, I praise you for the abundant life that you have given me as a result of your discomfort. Jesus paid for my pain so I don't have to and that is a reason to rejoice. I ask that you open my eyes to the opportunities to serve you, even if that means being uncomfortable sometimes. I ask for your strength and courage as different situations approach. You are my rock.

Straighten Up | Matthew 5:14-16

You are out on a run and there is not anyone around. You are feeling tired and you know your form is less than majestic. But you see other people and your posture straightens up as you manage to get a fresh breath of life. You cannot possibly let them see how you are sucking major air!

Or perhaps you are running a race. You are dying a little bit, but you are about to pass a group of supporters on the sideline. They cheer you on and you gain a new found energy as your shoulders drop, your arms return to a ninety-degree angle and your legs start moving at a normal pace.

I experienced this as I ran my first 5K on a 200-meter indoor track—25 laps. At the first mile I was fine, but things started hurting about the middle of the second mile. My form was breaking down and my pace was dropping off a little bit. But luckily, I had a multitude of cheerleaders along the final stretch of the track that would encourage me every time I went by. I found myself drifting into a slump on the backstretch, but every round I found a new burst of energy to improve my form. How would my race and time improved if I would have maintained my pace and good form the entire race, not just on the final stretch? I imagine it would have cut a good amount of time off.

How would your runs improve if you attempted to maintain good form and pace your entire run as opposed to just around the crowds? Do we fall into the "look good" trap in our lives? Put on a smile and be pleasant when we are around people?

Who you are when you are alone reveals your true character. Show Christ's love always, not just when you *should*. By constantly serving Christ with our lives, it won't take a conscious effort but it will become natural. Your form and pace becomes constant and your ability to abide in Christ flourishes because you're working to live in him always.

Dare | Hebrews 10:32-39

Starting out in the back of the pack may not give you the best chance at success. Sometimes you have to take the risk of failing in order to achieve the best possible outcome. You cannot fear failure for when little is weighed, little can be gained.

In Hebrews, the people are called to persevere in faith. The early Christians had no fear of persecution and stood up to adversity. But overtime, they started to "shrink back" and become complacent of the realities of the kingdom of God.

In order to receive the riches of the Lord, we must not step back but step up. We cannot submit to the condemnation of the world. The Lord does not condemn when we have accepted his Son and the gift of the Holy Spirit in our lives. We must learn to take the right risks in order to stand up for the truths of love, justice, and also grace.

Step up, step out, and seek the kingdom of God.

Lord, I realize that in order to follow you my life must look different than the rest of the world. I realize that following you is active, not passive. Show me the risks I should be taking daily and give me the boldness to pursue these opportunities. Thank you for taking the ultimate risk by offering your Son, the most important sacrifice that has redeemed my life and so many others.

Battle | Ephesians 6:10-20

On race day, do you ever approach the line in a mindset of battle? In high school there was a very vivid saying that our cross country team used: "Trample the weak. Hurdle the dead."

It resembles a war cry in my opinion.

We find competitive fire in gauging our energy into fervor and excitement. It is easier to find your competitive edge when you picture your competitors as the enemy.

The Christian life is also compared to a battle, but it is no cross country race. Satan, our enemy, is real, alive and active in our world, coming only to steal, kill, and destroy (John 10:10). God has equipped us with all that we need for our battle of spiritual warfare ahead. He has provided us with his armor of strength and it is our responsibility to accept the challenge and suit up.

Reflect: Which piece of God's holy armor stands out to you the most?

God, help me to realize the reality of the war that consumes our world each and every day. There are physical wars being fought and everyone acknowledges those, but few consider the eternal battle of this world. I may not be comfortable with the idea of fighting, but that does not mean I am going to stand down to the threats of Satan and the world. I am made strong because you are my strength, Lord. Equip me for the battle today.

Messenger | 1 Samuel 4:12-13

Are you familiar with the story of "Marathon" in which the marathon race was born? The fable is crafted in light of the main character Pheidippides, a Greek messenger. It is said that after the battle took place at the battlefield of Marathon, Pheidippides ran all the way to Athens to tell the people that the Greeks were victorious over the Persians. The story goes on that Pheidippides did not stop until he reached Athens which was the 26.2-mile distance. Upon reaching Athens, he proclaimed *nenikekamen* which means, "We have won." After his announcement, he fell over and died. Wow. Quite dramatic.

We are also messengers. In the Great Commission of Christ Jesus, we are called to go out and make disciples of all nations, telling them the good news of Jesus' death and resurrection. We are to go out proclaiming this message as if our life depended on it—with fervor and without ceasing.

Are we that much different than Pheidippides? We have the message of "we have won." It is not because of anything that we have done, but everything that has already been done. We don't fight the battle of sin and death, but our role is to proclaim the results of the battle: "We have won!"

Reflect: When is the last time that you have told someone about the good news of Jesus Christ in which there is victory? More importantly, how do you show it with the way you act and speak each day?

Correction | Proverbs 12:1

Drop your arms. Head up. Stride out. Kick now.

Advice from the wise often causes us to think mid-stride. Sometimes it is frustrating, while other times it can be helpful.

As runners, we drive our bodies into cooperation through training. It is then that our bodies become sensitive to discipline as they meet the command of our mind and spirit.

Our discipline becomes our knowledge. Through our own experiences and the guidance of others, we store up this knowledge. We are then enabled to make good choices and practice daily disciplines, producing more knowledge and strong habits for the future.

Ignoring the correction of past experience from yourself or others is called stupid in Proverbs. Solomon doesn't sugarcoat anything.

Allow yourself to grow and be shaped by correction, because in this there is long lasting wisdom. Humble yourself to hear words of correction as you seek daily disciplines on and off the training track.

God, discipline is hard, but I praise you that you help me through it. I know I can do nothing through my own strength, and I am so grateful that you choose to help your children through the wisdom of your scriptures, other people, and my own experiences. Don't let my life be one characterized by stupidity, but by wisdom. You are my guide. Guide me in the ways of your righteousness that I may pursue all that you have for me.

Ambassador | 2 Corinthians 5:20-21

In high school before our team walked off the bus into a restaurant or a meet, my coach would always say, "Remember who you are representing."

We did not only represent ourselves individually, but our team and our school. With that knowledge in mind, it was always easier for everyone to be on their best behavior. Everyone knew they were responsible for representing something greater than themselves.

Is it easier for you to put on a better attitude when you know you are representing your school, work, or any organization?

Sometimes we forget that we are representing our Heavenly Father all the time. We are not only responsible for representing ourselves, but we must work to carry out a clear representation of Christ in our lives.

In addition to representing Christ in our actions, we must be spokespeople of truth. When you are traveling with a group or team, it is common to proudly tell others who you are and where you are from; you are not ashamed of spreading the word and you might even like the attention.

We must carry this same mentality as we speak truth into the lives of our peers. We are on God's team (no matter how cliché that may sound). We are to represent Christ in word and in deed, always reflecting upon his grace and love in our lives.

Reflect: How are you representing Christ in your daily life? Are you proud of what you represent?

Help | Jude 1:24-25

It is hard to run a race alone. As you push your limits physically, mentally and emotionally. If you are lucky enough to have a training partner or teammate that encourages you during your workouts and races, you know the difference this makes. When you start to feel your breaths get heavy and the lactic acid seep through your veins, a little encouragement could make all the difference.

This is a beautiful example of the assistance God wants to offer you each moment of every day. He wants to build you up in the highs and the lows. He is always there, but we find in the times of weakness is when we need him the most.

We understand weakness at an intimate level. We know what it feels like to be on low battery yet still trying to operate at 110%. We have the opportunity to surrender in our weakness and allow God to fill us when we are drained of life (2 Cor. 12:9). He is there to be our partner of encouragement, our Lord of life and keep us motivated through every step that we take.

God, thank for being my constant breath of air and encouragement through the highs and the lows. I praise you for the simple fact that you take me and love me just as I am. I don't want to run the race alone. Help me to recognize your presence daily and be grateful for the people you have put in my life.

Visualize | Ephesians 2:1-9

Visualizing your race before race day is a helpful pre-race tactic as you imagine the turns, inclines and competition all around. You picture yourself owning the course and pursuing success right down to the final straightaway.

One of the most powerful visualization exercises I participated in involved laying on the floor in a dark room as the race was described to me piece by piece. It ended with, "You achieved your PR by over 10 seconds with a strong kick."

Notice the past tense. You *achieved.* When Paul is speaking to the Ephesians about the hope and life in Christ, he speaks in the past tense. He tells them they have been raised up and seated with Christ and it is by grace that you have been saved.

The Ephesians were not receiving a message about their saving for the future, but their saving in the present that has already occurred. They only had to accept it! There is freedom in knowing that the hard stuff is behind you and the debt has been paid. You have achieved. Now it is time to fully live.

Salvation is not something that can be earned, but can only be accepted as a gift.

Fast forward to the reality of you finishing the race. Oh, the relief. Past tense. It is *finished.* The hard work is done. Christ provides the ultimate visualization and confidence in completion that offers you a gateway of peace.

Praise God for the work he completed in his Son. Pray and meditate on John 17:3-5.

History | Deuteronomy 14:1-21

Keeping track of your running history is important. You know where you have been and that helps in pointing you to where you want to go. We keep training logs and remember instances of injury, good race strategy, bad race strategy, successful training plans, and personal plans of fueling your body. All of these things help construct a stronger premise for the future as you continue to grow and develop as a runner.

Christians have the privilege of a history found in Jewish people of the Old Testament. It tends to be easy to utilize only the New Testament when learning about your faith, but by doing this, the entirety of the Christian faith cannot be grasped. By knowing the Old Testament, the New Testament is made so much richer! The Old Testament offers a history for what the good news or gospel of the New Testament is based on. It offers biblical context and why Jesus came to earth. It demonstrates the world's desperate need for a savior as it also shows the multi-dimensionality of our God. The reality of God's anger is shown in light of his overflowing mercy and love. Sometimes we forget that the Old Testament or Hebrew Bible was the only Bible Jesus read from.

I encourage you to get familiar with the Old Testament. It is full of the legalistic law that we are free from under Christ Jesus, fascinating stories, prophecies, wisdom and praise.

Challenge: Read Isaiah 53. Do you see Jesus in fulfillment of this writing?

Pray and praise the Lord as you read Psalm 113.

Opposite | Romans 12:2

The runner's rules of the road instruct the runner to go against traffic in order to see the oncoming traffic. This way the runner avoids getting hit from behind as a result of not being able to see the traffic and react. When you are able to see what is coming towards you, you have more time to move yourself accordingly. When you take the risk and run with traffic at your back, you have to be constantly checking back over your shoulder for cars. This may slow you down, break up your stride, and it just gets annoying after awhile.

In Romans 12:2, you are told to "not conform to the pattern of this world, but be transformed by the renewing of your mind." We should not be running with traffic everyday, looking like everyone else. As a follower of Christ, you are to look different. We should be running against traffic to be able to gauge what is coming at us. When you are running with traffic at your back, you have a higher chance of being sideswiped and getting hurt.

Paul goes on to say in Romans that when our minds are transformed, we have the ability to discern what God's will is for our lives.

When you walk in the way of the Lord rather than the ways of the world, you are receptive to how your life should be lived. There are still dangers to running against traffic, but you have a greater ability to avoid preventable dangers.

Let us turn from the world and seek the benefits of running in the Lord's will for our lives.

My Counselor, thank you for transformation and being able to look different than everyone else in the world who chooses not to follow you. I admit that it is hard to be different, but with your strength, I can do all things. You have made me strong and courageous with mighty discernment. Prepare me for this day and the next as I approach the challenges that lie ahead.

Lessons from the Stumbling Series

God may get more glory on the bad days. Not meeting our own goals and expectations is a perfect reminder that we are not really capable of doing anything outside of the power of Christ. In fact, in John 15, Jesus straight up tells us that apart from him we can't do anything at all. Our identity must be found in him, not in our abilities to perform one way or another.

The following message was sent to me after my high school state race from a great friend and mentor, Sara. I pray this prayer for you as you feel like your falling or have already found yourself on the ground. God's grace is sufficient.

"While falling on your face is definitely not fun, it just points us right back to our need for HIM in everything, which is a good thing. I'm praying that this would be one more way he could show you that your worth is NOT found in your running, but in His unconditional love for you. He loves you no less after a bad race and no more after a stellar race. I think that this is a reminder that you need him. He will continue to use your life and your sport. That is an outstanding combo, my friend, and He will continue to put it to GREAT use for his purposes."

Root | Hebrews 10:8-14

An injury will never fully heal if you continue to "work through it." There are plenty of temporary fixes for your pain as you attempt to tape up, cross train, try new shoes, choose trails over concrete...But when there is a real injury, none of these are realistic, long-term fixes. You have to address the root.

Real injury often calls for time off, but we often veer away from that. We see the short-term effects like losing a couple days of workouts, instead of looking at the possibility of not being able to run for months. We hate to consider that a few days off could save months of pain and suffering. Ideally, we could eradicate all of those temporary fixes.

Before Jesus, the Jewish priests were responsible for laying down "a temporary fix" for the sin of the people. They sacrificed a pure animal in the name of the Lord in order to atone for the sins of the people. But in the book of Hebrews, Paul declares the freedom under the priest who offered the ultimate sacrifice: Jesus Christ.

This sacrifice is a one-time deal that covers the sin of those who believe in the hope of his resurrection. Because of this, we no longer need priests to offer sacrifices. Jesus addressed the root and granted salvation for anyone willing to accept his gift.

Reflect: Do you find yourself trying to personally "make up for" the sin in your life by doing good or going to church? Have you fully understood the magnitude of Jesus's sacrifice? Pray to live in the mentality of "not do, but done." Jesus is the only one that covers us.

Deliverance | 1 Corinthians 15:50-58

As we train and race, we are all longing for victory—victory translate into deliverance. Victory in running brings us bits of satisfaction, but never full contentment. The satisfaction is temporary and soon fades. Our true victory—our deliverance—is found in Christ alone.

Read this passage from 1 John 5:1-5 in a variety of ways (out loud, in your head, slowly, etc.). What stands out to you? What does victory mean for you?

"Everyone who believes that Jesus is the Christ is born of God, and everyone who loves the father loves his child as well. This is how we know that we love the children of God: by loving God and carrying out his commands. In fact, this is love for God: to keep his commands. And his commands are not burdensome, for everyone born of God overcomes the world. This is the victory that has overcome the world, even our faith. Who is it that overcomes the world? Only the one who believes that Jesus is the Son of God."

Looming | Philippians 4:4-9

What is your daunting workout?

In high school, mile repeats always had an ominous and infamous connotation. The day of mile repeats always loomed around. While I feared the pain they would bring, they were never as bad as I made them up to be in my mind.

While workouts seem so difficult before they begin, it becomes a matter of pushing through them in order to get the work done and feel the relief of completion at the end. Sometimes the workouts are not even as painful as they are monotonous. If you let yourself get lazy or distracted in the middle though, your workout can be compromised.

Some days can remind us of tough workouts. Some days hold great anticipation and even fear, but once the day plays out, it is not as bad as you thought it would be. While days may be long and difficult, but there is no point in stressing yourself out before it even happens. Stressing over one day only leaves a stressful anticipation for the next.

Reflect: Take days one at a time, approaching them with a spirit of peace that exists above your circumstances. When something controls your emotions, you begin to serve it. Remind yourself of who you serve and why.

"So then, banish anxiety from your heart and cast off the troubles of your body, for youth and vigor are meaningless" (Ecclesiastes 11:10).

Delight | John 10:7-10

When you tell someone you are going for a run, do you say "I get to run" or "I have to run"? If it is a "get to," kudos to you for your excitement to feel refreshed by some endorphins as you renew your mind and body. If it is "have to," you may or may not frame this as an obligation or duty. Perhaps it starts out as a drag, but by the end you are so glad that you "got to" run.

When you are giving something to your relationship with God, is it a "have to" or a "get to"? Church, Bible study, prayer, reading your Bible…God never wanted this to be an obligation, but a joy to live and serve him.

Our nature calls us to worship something and that something consumes our time and thoughts. Why not worship a God that offers joy even in suffering and blessings that we do not deserve? Maybe church is like running for you, the thought begins as a sour one, but by the end you are glad you were able to go to church.

If the thought of living for Christ seems like a "have to" obligation for you, I encourage you to restart and reframe who Jesus Christ of the Bible is. He did not call us into duty; in fact he freed us from duty! Rather, he has called us into delight to live abundantly with unspeakable joy.

God, transform my duty into delight. You have created me with the purpose to serve you and I ask that you would help me recognize that daily. I know you want my life to be filled with joy and I know I do too! Guide me in your joy.

Witnesses | Hebrews 12:1-3

As runners cross the finish line, they file through and watch the finish of the other runners. Then they cheer them on as they finish the race. The people that have finished the race know what the runners have been through and perhaps have the best insight on how to finish this race now.

Hebrews 12:1 offers us a picture of running into a stadium surrounded by the faithful finishers of the Bible that are listed in Hebrews 11 (Abel, Enoch, Noah, Abraham, Sarah, Isaac, Jacob, Joseph, Moses and his parents, etc.). As we run our race, we are surrounded by this great cloud of witnesses that have already run the race in good faith; they are waiting for our faithful finish.

And as verse two says, we fix our eyes on Jesus who was the perfect finisher. He has run his race and sits in the seat of victory in the stadium, watching every runner come across the finish line.

Let us take the example of our faithful witnesses and pursue God even when we are not sure how or what will come of it. The writer of Hebrews highlights people who saw the reward of the faithfulness in their lifetimes and some that did not. Regardless, both rested on the promises of the Lord and trusted Him.

God, teach me from the example of your faithful servants what it means to run the race with perseverance. Guide me in what it means to fix my eyes on Jesus, learning from his joy and sharing in his victory. Thank you for his perfect finish that covers me when I stumble. Your grace is enough. Please teach me how to walk in your ways that I may seek your will.

Results | Proverbs 12:11

In order to see results, you must put forth the effort to pursue them. In a society that puts everything at our fingertips, running brings us back to the beginning. We must start from scratch and personally work our way up in order to achieve any goal. It is easy to dream about our goals or talk about them, but unless you put one foot in front of the other, you will never see any results.

We must turn from the "potentiality talk" and embrace the toughness of the action. In everything you do, do it as if working for the Lord (Col. 3:23). He deserves your best work, so leave your pride aside and strive for the best you have to offer.

Stop talking about what you could be doing to give, serve, love, or grow in your relationship with the Lord, but take a step forward. Mere talk does not bring any results; if something is tugging on your heart to make a change or make a difference, explore the pursuit of that pull today.

God, I am ready to put my life in action for the service of your kingdom. Your kingdom come, your will be done on earth as it is in heaven. It is easy to talk about potential, but it is a whole other task to put potential in motion. I am ready to surrender to seeking and serving you in all that I do so others may be filled with you.

"All hard work brings a profit, but mere talk leads only to poverty" (Proverbs 14:23).

All for One | 1 Corinthians 12:4-11

"YOUR ARMS ONLY MOVE AS FAST AS YOUR LEGS! SO MOVE THOSE ARMS!"

As you run, your arms are moving in the opposite direction of your legs, which may sound wrong until you try to run with the same arm and same leg. If you have never tried this before, you MUST try it. This rhythm of opposite leg and opposite arm is essential in order to run efficiently and the faster you crank your arms, the faster your legs will follow.

In 1 Corinthians 12, Paul speaks of the different kinds of spiritual gifts that each person is given, but "in all of them and in everyone it is the same God at work" (v. 6). If everyone was doing the same thing in the body of Christ, we wouldn't go anywhere.

Just as it is essential for the arms to be doing something different than the legs, the people in the body of Christ must fulfill different tasks to make the body function. The best part of it all is that we may be working on different tasks, but the work being done is all for the King of Kings and Lord of Lords.

Be encouraged by the unique difference you are making in the kingdom of God. You hold a unique purpose and praise God for the beauty and diversity of his kingdom that we may reach peoples of all nations.

Challenge: Read all of 1 Corinthians 12. Praise God for your unique abilities of what you have to offer the body of Christ in your pocket of the world. God has created you specifically to impact the world for his kingdom.

Handiwork | Ephesians 2:1-10

I'm sure you have a number of talents, hobbies, and abilities, but God has gifted you with the desire and ability to run. While most *can* run, you are unique in that God has given you the ability to find some gratification in it.

Love it or hate it… God crafted you as a runner. You are his perfectly crafted handiwork.

When you are responsible for creating something or coming up with an idea, how proud are you? You campaign for the purpose of your creation and want to see it succeed. You take pride in it and when it fulfills its purpose, you are filled with joy. Oh the joy that God is filled with when he sees us, his handiwork, fulfilling our purpose, which is ultimately living for him. Our running can be an agent for the fulfillment of both our joy and the Lord's joy.

How are you fulfilling your purpose as God's special piece of handiwork? Take time to pray and mediate on your runs. When you are running with a group, make a point to listen and encourage your fellow runners. You have a unique platform—do not squelch any opportunities.

Lord, I praise you for making me a runner. Thank you for the satisfaction I gain from being able to run anywhere and anytime, testing the skills and abilities that you have blessed me with. I know that the satisfaction that I gain from running is only a very small part of why you have created me as a runner. You have created me to serve those around me as I speak truth and life from your Word and my experience with you. Give me the words to say when I speak about you—let them be yours and not mine. Lord, I know your might cannot be put to shame (Acts 6:10).

Refresh | 2 Corinthians 5:17-21

Oh the beauty of the mid-race "second wind."

What prompts yours? A water stop to refresh your dry throat or splash your face? A Gu-pack? A friend or family member cheering you on? Simply reminding yourself of your training and goals?

Whatever yours is, you know it has the power to make you feel new. It gives you the power to forget what is behind and strive to what is before you. The "second wind" is not always reliable though. You can hope and pray, but some days it just won't be there.

But here we find the magnificence of Christ: he makes each day new for us. Because of his mercy and grace we do not have to live in guilt but we can experience joy even in hardship. This is always reliable.

We have the gift of a second wind each day. God is waiting to give this to you, you just have to ask for it. Ask for renewal and believe in its power. And thank God, it does not depend on our goodness, but on the perfect performance of his Son on the cross.

Reflect on these scriptures: Isaiah 43:18-29, Lamentations 3:22-24, & Ezekiel 36:26-28

Not by Us | Deuteronomy 8:10-18

Praise the Lord for your victory. Do not fall victim to conceit or pride by thinking you completed your victory alone. If that becomes your mindset, you risk falling into the trap that the Lord warned the Israelites against.

Let me frame Deuteronomy 8:10-18 in the eyes of our running context today...

When you have run and are satisfied, praise the Lord and warn your heart against pride. Let us never say, "My power and the strength of my hands (or my legs) have produced this wealth for me" (v. 17).

All things are given through the hands of the Lord and he deserves our praise regardless of the circumstances because he is the God who gives and takes away.

Let our satisfaction come from praising the Lord, because we can always praise him. When our satisfaction is only found in physical victory, we live unsatisfied and in search of something else to worship. True victorious satisfaction can only be found in the Lord.

God, thank you for the gift of being able to be satisfied and sustained in you. I praise you that my joy is not based on my circumstances, but in the constant victory that you grant me.

Overcome | John 16:33

Jesus makes us a promise in John 16:33.

We will encounter *thilpsei*. This is the Greek word for troubles, hardships, afflictions, distresses, and pressures. There is no doubt if we will encounter these troubles—they are definite. But he offers us peace in his reassurance that he has overcome the world that is full of all of these struggles.

While situations are overwhelming and seem like more than we can handle, it is encouraging to know that God is bigger.

When your obstacles (pain, anxiety, crazy emotions and trials) feel like more than you can handle, "Take Heart!" Jesus commands you to be courageous. He has conquered any and every obstacle that you have experienced, you are experiencing and you will experience. He is greater and he allows you to experience victory through him.

Reflect: If we are to conform to the image of Christ daily, what does that look like? How did Jesus act through the last day of his crucifixion—the ultimate trial? He submitted to God's will. He did not protest, complain or grumble even though the pain and struggle was unbearable. He faced the death we all deserve, so now we can rejoice in our sufferings for nothing compares to the brutality of this Roman execution.

Dear Father, you sent your Son to earth to endure the sin and the shame of this world. You understand the brokenness of this world better than anyone, so in the moments I am asking "Why God?" please comfort me. Speak to my heart, Lord. Tell me you understand as you offer a peace that transcends all understanding (Phil. 4:7). You are big in my brokenness and while I am small, you are so strong. Thank you for your might, God.

Lighten Up | Hebrews 12:1-3

Do you look forward to lightening up your gear on race day? Do you switch from your training clothes to a lighter singlet? Do you change from your trainers into your racing flats or spikes? When you lighten your load you are prepared for the race ahead. Becoming lighter and freer does not make the pain go away, but it is better than having weights tied around your feet. You are ready to run in freedom!

The writer of Hebrews tells us that we are to "throw off everything that hinders and the sin that so easily entangles" as we run the race of life (v. 1). We physically know the joys of throwing off heavy sweatshirts and sweatpants to run easier.

This is what it feels like to cast off and turn away from the sin that once held us captive in our lives. We no longer have to worry about carrying our sweatshirt or tying it around our waist.

We are able to throw the weights of this world off of our shoulders and onto the God of the universe because his Son paid the ultimate price of our sin on the cross. He bared the weight of the world as he sunk down in separation from God, but he conquered the grave and left all of our sin in the depths of hell. We can cast our cares upon the Lord because he cares for us (1 Pet. 5:7).

Now we have victory as we finish the race free of our burdens. Now we may sing, "Oh, death, where is your sting? Oh, hell, where is your victory?" (1 Cor. 15:55-57).

God, I praise you for your grace that lightens my soul as it sings, "Bless the Lord." Forgive me for not trusting in you completely, thinking that you are not big enough for my problems. Open my heart to trust you with anything and everything. I am ready to lighten my load and surrender to your will in exchange for your peace and love.

Daily Training Thought: Purpose

Meditate on this passage today from 1 Corinthians 9:24-27:

"Do you not know that in a race all the runners run, but only one gets the prize? Run in such a way as to get the prize. Everyone who competes in the games goes into strict training. They do it to get a crown that will not last, but we do it to get a crown that will last forever. Therefore I do not run like someone running aimlessly; I do not fight like a boxer beating the air. No, I strike a blow to my body and make it my slave so that after I have preached to others, I myself will not be disqualified for the prize."

What stands out to you? What words or phrases?

Do you find yourself competing daily for a crown that will not last or a crown that will last forever?

How are you focusing and living purposefully?

Nature | Galatians 5:13-26

My high school coach used to ease some nerves, but also pump us up by telling us "compete and time will take care of itself." He told us if we just put ourselves out there that our natural competitive nature would kick in and our goals would be achieved in the meantime. It is easy to get nervous when thinking about goals and when thinking too much, nerves are enough to psych you out completely.

We often put pressure on ourselves to produce results that we know we are capable of. But sometimes you need to stop thinking and instead draw confidence from your training and take the race head on with your other competitors. The rest will fall into place.

Christians are easy targets when it comes to worrying about the process rather than just living! When you are walking in the ways of the Lord and abiding (or "making your home") in Christ, the details and actions of your life will fall into place. When you have gained experience and knowledge, you don't have to worry about the "what ifs." When we are living a life saturated in the love and sacrifice of Jesus Christ, we are given a new nature that will produce spiritual fruit naturally.

So the same way in which our competitive nature reveals itself when the time comes, so will our desire to act kindly, joyfully, and patiently. Being good and loving should not be your goal in life, but simply seeking Christ in worship with your life; the fruit of the Spirit (love, joy, peace, patience, kindness, goodness, faithfulness, gentleness, and self-control) will take care of itself (v. 22-23).

Remind yourself of this today:
Live seeking the Lord and love will take care of itself.

Mind & Body | Romans 12:1

As runners, we are familiar with how important the connection is between the mind and the body. To be a good runner, you have to master the cooperation of the two together.

This is in complete contrast to what the Greek philosophers of Paul's time thought. In the realm of their spirituality, they believed in the importance of the mind but not the body. They often called for a separation of the two, highlighting the evils of the body.

But we cannot separate the mind and body. God created them both and we must care for both of them together—our running careers would not be successful if we neglected one or the other.

During Jesus' time, there was no separation of secular and sacred for the Jewish people. Everything worked together and not one without the other. Throughout the years and especially in our modern society, the two have been pulled completely apart. Your relationship with the Lord should impact every piece of your life as does every piece of your life should impact your relationship with the Lord. We understand the importance of a holistic experience and our souls crave to reunite the secular and sacred in one piece under God.

Our Heavenly Creator, thank you for the creation of these incredible bodies. You created my bones strong enough to withstand the running, but light enough to let me move freely. I recognize that the mind and body are equally important as I live to glorify you in all I do. Help me carry this same mentality of unity into my life as I bridge the gap between secular and sacred—everything I do is for you and under you. You are so deserving of my praise.

Check or Wreck | 1 Corinthians 11:27-32

We have all had those days where you begin your run and your stomach drops. You prepare yourself for a whole other kind of runs. There are the days that you stop immediately in the bathroom and take care of business. After that, all is resolved and you can move on. But then there are the days when there just isn't time to stop or you think, "Ah, it will move along." By the middle or the end of your run (if you actually make it), you may be singing a different tune. Your body feels like it has been twisted and turned and discomfort is an understatement. You then come to the thought, "I should have just stopped at the beginning and taken care of it."

I would like to call this the pre-run "check yourself before you wreck yourself."

Now let's get spiritual. I apologize for the grossness of that example.

Communion is a time to reaffirm your relationship with Jesus Christ, the Savior of the world. Communion looks different for everyone at different churches or personal quiet times. This is not something to be taken lightly, but we often get in the habit of taking communion routinely instead of wholeheartedly. It is your responsibility to clear your heart and your mind at the feet of Jesus before you partake in such an important act.

Verse 27 clearly says, "whoever eats the bread or drinks the cup of the Lord in an unworthy manner will be guilty of sinning against the body and blood of the Lord." Paul says to examine yourself. Rid your heart of vengeance, jealously, and all the hatred that is ungodly for if you partake in communion with evil in your heart, you only bring judgment on yourself.

Therefore, I return to my point: Check yourself before you wreck yourself.

Read and reflect on the Last Supper with Jesus and the disciples in Luke 22:14-23.

Reflect: When you enter into a time with the Lord, lay everything before him whether it be a sin in need of forgiveness or a praise in need of saying. God already knows all of your thoughts (Ps. 139:2), but by confessing them, you are recognizing what is happening in your life. It puts your heart and your head on the same page and brings you into a place of freedom and surrender.

God, you know my heart and I lift up to you the brokenness inside of me…

In Everything | Colossians 3:23-25

Everything we do is an act of worship, it is just a matter of what we are worshipping. In Colossians 3:23, we are told to do everything as if working for the Lord—everything as if serving the Lord.

Worship is derived from two words in the Bible. The first word is a physical representation as one kneels, bows, or puts his or hers face to the ground in a movement of respect or submission. The second one in translated into serving. Both of these words come back to a self-sacrificial action, saying that something or someone is greater than you are.[4]

We have the opportunity to run as worship in the same that we sing, play instruments, read scripture and listen to sermons. We can preach the gospel through the action of our running. First of all, God has made us as his creations in his image; when we do something worthy of glory, we can then point the glory to him. Without his creation of us and without him living in us, we would have no means to do what we do.

We also have the opportunity to run in freedom—making this a demonstration of the freedom we have to live in each new day. When you run in a way that God is glorified above yourself, you are worshipping in a way God intended you to run and live.

God, as I run today, reveal to me what it means to worship you in my running. Worship is all about you—remind me I have to remove myself from the equation in order to fully worship you. You are glorified when you alone receive glory. Then I can learn what it means to only boast you in God, for you are the God that gives and takes away. I never underestimate your power for you are sovereign over all.

Pack | Hebrews 10:23-25

As you run alongside the road, you put yourself at risk. There is no denying that when you run with other people you make yourself more noticeable to cars driving by. Not only are you more visible, but you have at least another pair of eyes and ears being attentive to the road for traffic. Someone may hear or see a car coming that you did not hear and notify the group to take action.

Running in a pack may involve the risk of being accountable for a bigger group on the road, but there are also great benefits.

As you follow Christ and his teachings, doing life in a pack resembles a similar situation. As you are out running against traffic by yourself, it would be easy for an oncoming car to lose sight of you in the horizon. When you are trying to live out the Christian walk on your own, it is more difficult than if you find yourself encouraged and surrounded by a group of fellow believers. If you are running in a pack, the driver of the car is more likely to see a group of runners and act accordingly. In the group you have more eyes, ears and mouths to keep you accountable and aware of what is going on around you (good or bad).

By doing life in a group that loves you and keeps you accountable, you have a greater chance of faithful survival. It doesn't make it easy, but it makes it easier when you able to work together as a team. You do not have to run the race alone—there are so many people who are willing to run it with you, side-by-side.

Praise God if you have people in your life that support you along the way as you grow in faith together. If you are trying to navigate your faith on your own, ask God to show you people who are seeking him like you are. God will help you in providing faithful friends, but you have to make an effort to seek them also.

Give | 1 Timothy 6:17-19

Runners understand the concept of giving in sacrifice in order to receive something greater. The more you give to your training the more you are prepared to get from it. You are placing an investment in your fitness and your future goals by preparing your mind, body and spirit for the race ahead.

The poor widow in Mark 12:41-44 understood the concept of giving. She gave out of her poverty and expected nothing in return. She laid down her little money to reap benefits that she could not tangibly receive in that moment. We are called to give just as the widow gave, expecting nothing in return.

As followers of Christ, we are called not to just give of our time and our talents but our resources. Whether rich or poor, all are to give generously. A generous giver will gain great abundance (Prov. 11:24). Giving must come from a place of cheer, because God loves a cheerful giver (2 Cor. 9:7). While it is sometimes difficult to give because you do not see the immediate fruit of your giving, God sees it and will reward you. Do not give that all may see you, but let it be an intimate fellowship between you and the Father in secret (Matt. 6:2-4).

Take a chance of giving all to the mission of the kingdom, because God took a chance on you. Allow God to work in your giving and his blessing (see Malachi 3:10).

God, thank you for the ultimate gift of your Son on the cross. I know I can never give enough to pay you back and I praise you that this is not the reason I give. I give out of thankfulness and I pray my heart and mind would continue learning what it means to be a cheerful giver. As Christians we are called to meet the physical needs of those around us so they might see you—God, guide me to where my resources should be given to impact your kingdom.

Normality | 1 Thessalonians 5:16-19

When a runner is able to run free from injury, it is easy to take that for granted. That is until injury strikes. Then you find yourself longing for the "normality" of running again. We assume that our normal state is to be in movement, when we were never guaranteed that. We often view running as a right rather than a privilege.

Similarly, we live our lives in a state of normal when there is ease and simplicity. When something goes awry, we pray ourselves back into "normality." We view our lives of "things going right" as a right rather than a privilege.

It's time for a paradigm shift.

We must live in a mindset that our normal state is injury—our brokenness. This does not result in a lifestyle of victimization and apathy, but it would call for us to constantly rejoice in the freedom of running and daily living.

We cannot take the gifts given to us for granted. Rejoicing cannot be reserved for the moments we return from injury or a hard time in our lives—rejoicing should be constant as we pray continually and giving thanks in everything.

God, thank you for the ability to run and live freely. Remind me daily that life is a gift that should not be taken for granted. I pray that I can live boldly in my brokenness, because you are the one that has saved me from the wages of sin. I will boast in you alone, Lord, because you are the King in which all things are under.

Shift | Titus 2:11-15

It is easy to be the critic and point out everything that is wrong. Everything that is too hot or too cold. Everything that is painful. Everything you feel is moving in spite of you. It takes a different perspective to seek the blessings of this world and offer them up in thanksgiving every instant. This is worship.

Do not dare confine your worship to singing at the church service or the weekend retreat. Living in constant worship of the Creator changes everything because it is no longer about you.

Shifting your perspective from victim to victor is the difference between living of the world to living in the world. Our victory is not found in anything that we have done, but in the perfection of a perfect Savior that died so that we may live and find joy even in our pain.

We must strive to be a piece in the world rather than a product of the world. Living in love above the world's wavering circumstances is the key to living victoriously in Jesus.

Lord, thank you for giving me the opportunity to worship you in everything I do. I pray that my life is glorying to you as I shine the light of Christ to all who I encounter. I know you can make a difference through me so I offer myself as a living sacrifice for the work of your kingdom.

Carry Me | Isaiah 46:3-5

Have you met "the wall"? Have you been in the spot where your legs feel like jelly as if you could melt on the road? The cry of your heart becomes, "Carry me, God!"

Before you can walk, before you can crawl, you must pull yourself into a place of total surrender. Your training and food fuel only pulls you so far sometimes before God becomes your only source of energy.

When things get tough, the cry of a child's heart is to be carried by their father. Their impulse is to raise their hands and call for their dad. "Abba, Father!"

Your Heavenly Father is waiting to carry you. He is only waiting for your call (see James 4:8).

When you are a child, you cannot do anything on your own. You depend on your parents to take care of you. God longs for us to return to a state of spiritual dependency that is entirely on him. We need to return to a childlike faith not to become immature, but dependent on our Father. We need to understand that we cannot do life without him. He is ready and willing to carry and comfort us, encourage us, and make us into his Holy Nation.

Heavenly Father, I surrender. I want to depend on you through the good and the bad. I know you are waiting on my call, so Lord humble my heart so I can cry out to you. My soul yearns for you while the world often pulls me away from you. Guide me in my search for you.

Fuel | 1 Corinthians 6:19-20

Fueling the athlete's body should be a sport within itself. There are so many plans for daily eating, pre-race eating, and post-race eating. Overall, an athlete's simple responsibility should be to take care of the body.

We forsake the seriousness of Jesus' sacrifice on the cross when we treat our bodies poorly by under-eating or over-eating. When Jesus died for our sins, Paul tells us in 1 Corinthians that our *bodies* have been bought at a price (v. 20).

This is a priceless purchase and we often neglect the weightiness of it.

If you were to buy a Ferrari, you would fuel it with the best gas—the gas that it was intended to take. You wouldn't dare fuel it up with a gallon of orange juice! You paid way too much to obstruct the insides and let the engine go bad.

You may have spent your life's savings on the car, but weigh that against the price that Jesus paid on the cross. He put his own life on the line to purchase yours. The least we can do is protect his investment in us.

Find out your best fuel—the fuel you were intended to take.

Reflect: How do you fuel your body? Are you able to honor God by the way you eat—consuming fruits and vegetables, not just junk? Praise God for the natural foods that he gives us right from the ground! Also, do not forget that self-discipline is a fruit of the Spirit while gluttony is a sin. How can you better serve God by preserving the body he has given you?

Foolishness | 1 Corinthians 1:18-19

I will never understand how you run so much.

I will never understand how you run so far.

I will never understand how you run so fast.

Do you hear that as you navigate your running career?

How you do it is one question, but do you ever get the "Why?"

To people who do not understand running, it seems like a nonsense world of pain, time and effort. People who do not run will probably never understand why you spend as much energy as you do on it. It comes across as foolishness to "outsiders," but to you, it is inspiring and life-giving.

Non-Christians experience a similar struggle for understanding. People who don't have a relationship with Christ see the Christian life as crazy business. They see the Bible as a book of rules rather than a book of life. Just as it says in 1 Corinthians, "the message of the cross is *foolishness* to those who are perishing, but to us who are being saved, it is the power of God" (v. 18).

Sometimes I want to say to "non-runners," just dip your toes in the water and you will understand the joys that running can bring to your life. The same goes for those resistant to a life of following Christ; dip your toes in the water and watch the foolishness transform itself into an experience of wonder and life.

Dear Lord, thank you for the cross. Sometimes it doesn't make sense to me, but God, I praise you that your acceptance is not based on my understanding. The cross represents your saving grace and ultimate love that you pour out on me daily. You redeemed the torture of the cross and that is not foolishness to me. Help me to be bold when my strength is failing, remembering that you are my only King worth pleasing.

Turn Around | Philippians 3:12-14

When you run out and down a trail not knowing where you are going, it is easy to feel like you could be running down that path forever. You begin second guessing which way to turn or how far you should run down before turning back. But then when it's time to turn around and return on the path you came, it doesn't feel like you went as far as you first thought. While the path was first unknown and felt so far, the known path seems shorter and you become more confident in your destination.

The beauty of life in Christ is that before him, you were running down a path that wasn't certain and it felt as if it could go on forever with no end in sight. But you have made your turn around. You know where you have been and now know where you are going. You have confidence in the path ahead and while you might not be sure of what you could encounter along the way, you know your goal.

There is no longer a fear of the unknown, but you can be confident by trusting in the Lord. You can enjoy the path and have your mind fixed on what is ahead rather than what is behind. You are able to run the path in freedom. Praise God for the freedom you have in Christ.

Reflect: Meditate on the greatness of God and what it means to follow his will when you walk in his ways.

"This is what the LORD says-- your Redeemer, the Holy One of Israel: "I am the LORD your God, who teaches you what is best for you, who directs you in the way you should go" (Isaiah 48:17).

Strategy | Matthew 4:12-17

Our God is a God of strategy. This is an awesome concept to me, because as runners we believe in strategy whether it is in pre-race preparation or race day execution. This affirms yet again that we are made in the image of God himself and reflect his qualities unto the world (Gen. 1:27).

You may be asking, "How is God strategic?" Let me give you just one example.

The ancient land of Israel held one of the most traveled trade routes of the ancient Middle East called the International Coastal Highway. This stretched from Egypt to Mesopotamia. The highway was situated far from Jerusalem as the road followed the coast of the Mediterranean Sea up through the Galilee.

Where was the ministry of Jesus situated primarily? In the Galilee! Jesus did not go to the city of Jerusalem and give his message only for the Jewish people. Jesus lived in Capernaum, a town along the highway as it passed up towards Damascus.

The message of the kingdom was not reserved for the Jewish people, but it was for the Gentiles, which can also be translated "all the nations." Jesus was not born to a family in Jerusalem, but he grew up in Nazareth in the Galilee.

This message of Jesus was intended for travelers, for fishermen, and therefore the world. Strategic indeed.

God, you are sovereign over all and I thank you for including me in your master plan. Help me to take lessons of strategy with me daily whether I am on the course or interacting with my friends. I pray that I can be more like you and I praise you for the strategy you choose to carry out in my life every day.

Spirit & Truth | John 4:23-26

Have you met a runner who has all the aspirations to be a great runner, but does not act on it? Or have you met someone with a lot of natural talent, but does not care to work hard or have any drive to pursue their potential?

The best runner is going to have a fine mixture of both of these characteristics. You cannot have one without the other. Leaning on one may get you somewhere, but not as far as if you embrace both.

Jesus tells the woman at the well in John 4 that "the time will come when the *true* worshipers will worship in spirit and in truth" (v. 24). True worshippers will bring forth praise by using not just their heart and not just the head, but both of them together.

You must bring together your desire, your zeal and attentive nature which gives life to you, your body, and the body of Christ; at the same time, you must hold on to the gospel truth of Jesus's death and resurrection. (For references to "word of truth," see Colossians 1:5, Ephesians 1:13, James 1:18.)

Jesus is truth (John 14:6).

When referencing "being filled with the Holy Spirit," it is common to think of a wild or crazy person. When in reality, the fruit of the Spirit is actually one of self-control. The Spirit of God in you embraces vivacity, while holding the truth of Jesus Christ as the compass.

Reflect: What does it look like to balance in spirit and in truth? If worship is a daily act, are spirit and truth featured daily in your life?

The Son | Proverbs 4:18-19

Have you been on those runs where the sun is in your eyes and it is nearly blinding? It makes it impossible to see too far ahead because you are squinting to secure your next steps. In the heat, you can feel really the intensity of its rays.

Next time you are being blinded by the sun, be reminded of the glory of the Son.

Oh, how we should live in a state of being blinded by the Son! We should focus on the road right in front of us, avoiding the pain and difficulty of trying to look too far ahead.

Sometimes your most difficult runs happen in the presence of the shining sun. They are refining races and grueling workouts. Rejoice in these experiences of growth just as God continues to form you and shape you in the glaring presence of his Son.

And let me remind you that just because you cannot always feel the brightness of the rays does not mean that the sun is not there. The sun is always shining despite our ability to see or feel it.

From the rising of the sun to the place where it sets, the name of the Lord is praised (Ps. 113:3). Your Son rises with us each day and you are never far. God, you are the alpha and omega, beginning and end, who shines on us in the good and the bad. I praise you for the warmth of the sun and the healing and growth it offers to the earth. Thank you for your healing and restorative ways that lead me in the message and love of your Son.

Lessons from the Stumbling Series

One night I was running with a group of people at the forest preserve. As usual there were tons of roots, sticks and holes that were an open invitation for a twisted ankle or fall. That night there was also a lot of mud—more hazard.

We got through the run with no problems. A few people went towards the boat ramp to put their feet in the water and chill out. One person eases her feet into the water as she walks down the boat ramp and then…WHAM!

She wipes out and conveniently catches herself on her right arm. It just *looked* painful. Someone said, "Isn't it amazing we can make it through an hour run with no problems, but the second we relax—accidents happen."

How often does this happen? We are working hard to be in tune with the teachings of Jesus and the second we relax, accidents happen. The second we let the guard to our hearts down, we become vulnerable. Satan never rests, so he is always ready to pounce.

When we can live in a state of conscience belief, confidence in the Lord and what Jesus has done, Satan knows we are a threat to his empire. We must be aware that he is real and looks to destroy. Let us live in the refuge of our God and King always.

"Be alert and of sober mind. Your enemy the devils prowls around like a roaring lion looking for someone to devour. Resist him, standing firm in faith, because you know that the family of believers throughout the world is undergoing the same king of sufferings.

And the God of all grace, who called you to his eternal glory in Christ, after you have suffered a little while, will himself restore you and make you strong, firm and steadfast. To him be the power forever and ever. Amen" (1 Pet. 5:8-11).

Gift | Psalm 100

Have you ever stopped in awe of being able to run? Do you praise God for the gift that has been given to you? There are some people who can't or who really just don't like to run.

Running is the gift that keeps on giving as it brings life and health to your body, renewal of the mind, fellowship, and goals for each new day.

Make a purpose of lifting up a prayer of thanksgiving before and after each run. No run is guaranteed so we should never take a day for granted.

God, thank you for waking me up this morning. Sleeping is a mere act of trust as I surrender my awareness to rest my body to be ready for today. For some reason, you have created me as a runner and I praise you for that. Forgive me for ever taking advantage of the ability to run. I want my life to be honoring to you and I know you have given me the unique ability to glorify you in my running. Teach me what it means to glorify you in running as I learn and grow as your child.

Practice | Colossians 4:2-6

Strides before and after runs serve a few different purposes. Before your race, a stride warms up the body and prepares the body for the pace that it will soon encounter. A stride after a run builds muscle memory for the future as you kick up the pace on already fatigued legs.

By giving your body a glimpse of the race pace throughout your workout routines, you are preparing yourself for the actual race. You are working to build a new realm of comfortable as you push the pace into the memory of your body's mind and muscles.

We can build spiritual disciplines as we refine the conscience of our mind, body and soul, preparing us for the daily race that we run. You build yourself into a new realm of life by practicing prayer often and rejoicing always (1 Thess. 5:16-17). Start making habits to grow spiritually by simply thanking God for waking up in the morning and asking him to reveal himself to you in this day.

When you see people along the street, pray for them. When a friend, family member or acquaintance pops into your mind, pray for them. The Spirit of the Lord works in beautiful ways to remind you and guide you; therefore, acknowledge your thoughts and use them as footnotes from God himself. After all, we, the earth, are his footstool in which his reign is over and above (Isa. 66:1).

Lord, your ways are higher than my ways and your thoughts higher than my thoughts (Isa. 55:9). Guide me in the ways of your Spirit, as you love me in grace, truth and mercy. I want to be more like you as I throw off the ways of this world. Remind me that each day is new and I have been created new in you.

Perfection | Hebrews 12:1-3

Running is a beautiful thing. There can still be victory without winning!

Let's frame a marathon for example. Everyone that finishes celebrates the achievement with their fellow racers and is rewarded with a medal at the end. We have the opportunity to be victorious in the race when we are running the race behind perfection. That is Jesus.

Everyone sees his finish and rejoices in his accomplishment as millions of runners finish the race in light of his work. No one can measure up to the perfection of Jesus although they might finish the race well.

Every runner faces his or her challenges along the way. In a race, they battle negative thoughts, cramping muscles and dehydration. The importance is in finishing the race though. There is victory in crossing the finish line knowing that you did the best you could do.

Rejoice in the perfect path Jesus has carved, and try your best to navigate his will that has been poured out on your life's race.

God, you sent perfection to pave the way for me so I wouldn't have to be perfect and I praise you for that. I will strive to follow your will with all I have but I realize that I will still fall short. Thank you for your grace and your strength in my weakness. Let me look towards Jesus, the perfect finisher, to refine my race strategy and pursue you with my whole heart.

Road | James 1:2-8

Each one of us has our own road with holes all along. Everyone's road is different, but equally broken. Our holes are created by sin like worry, pride, selfishness, and greed. These holes give us a reason to stumble and break stride.

We long to run without stumbling, but we cannot fix our roads on our own.

God is our master builder who is responsible for closing us down in order to build us up stronger. He wants to make the road good as new, but we often throw barriers up at each end. We block his entrance. He is ready to fix the road, but he cannot get through until you allow him through.

God rejoices in the holes for in our gaps, he fills our souls. Without these holes, he would have no reason to encounter you on the road at all. Perfect people have no need for a healer.

He is ready to repair you, one pothole at a time; he is just waiting for you to take down the barriers and allow him free passage. Times of repair are difficult and sometimes inconvenient, but they are so worth it when the road is complete.

Reflect: What are your potholes? Do you take down the boundaries and allow God to work on your heart?

God, thank you for being a God who cares enough to fix me in my brokenness. I surrender the boundaries I put up around my heart and soul. I pray that your Spirit would transform me.

Like a Child | Luke 18:15-17

If you have ever been around young kids as they run a race, there is so much to learn. I love cheering for kids who are new to racing because they are so incredibly receptive to what you are telling them. Especially for their first race, they don't know what they are getting themselves into so they just get out there and run their hearts out. They don't get inside their own heads and become overcome with nerves, but they run to win. There is no fear! Perhaps we need to take some of their characteristics with us: dropping our fears and the complexity of exact mile splits and simply run the race!

Similarly to running, there is a lot we can learn from children in the realm of our faith. Jesus told the people that no one will enter the kingdom of God unless they have faith like a child. Children aren't picking apart their faith, but embracing it. They are not overly skeptical of the story of Jesus, but they trust the miracles of the Bible. How often do we begin to over-analyze the truth of Bible and we miss the message of the gospel entirely? There is no problem with details and questions of faith, but when these questions overshadow the power and life of Jesus Christ, there is an issue; you are no longer serving God, but you are serving the skepticism.

As human beings we want exact answers and when we don't have them, we feel as if we are being scammed. Sorry to say it, but no one has all the answers of this faith. Not even the angels fully understand the message of the gospel (1 Pet. 1:12)! Take a leap of faith and trust in the Creator of the Universe. We often say we need to see proof—well, look around on your next run… God's incredible creation surrounds you everyday.

God, bring me into a place of faith that is not self-serving, but self-sacrificial. I want to serve you, embracing what it means to have faith like a child. Teach me how to run free and live free for you, and you alone.

Inspiration | Mark 5:18-20

Do you find motivation in inspirational stories? They could be stories of teammates helping each other across the finish line or a dad pushing his son in his wheelchair through 1000+ races (www.TeamHoyt.com). It is amazing how personal testimonies and stories offer us hope and a renewed strength that says, "You can do it!"

Has someone inspired you in your running career?

Who has encouraged you or inspired you in relationship with Christ? Is there someone who has seemed to go above and beyond as an example to you? *Really think about it.*

Finding people who inspire and motivate you are essential to continual growth in your spiritual journey. God is always moving and by sharing stories in fellowship and discipleship, the body of Christ has an incredible opportunity to impact one another. Edification comes through personal experience.

Share your struggles and the beauty of what God is doing in and through your life with others. You never know if what you have gone through or what you are going through could inspire or encourage someone else in their life. Also, be willing and able to listen to other people's journeys to find personal support. God has knitted our world together in incredible ways as we act as his love to one another.

Dear Lord, you are my inspiration. You have inspired me with your selfless love, continual sacrifice and guidance. Because of the great inspiration you are, I want your love to transpire through me so I may inspire others. God, provide opportunities for me to be your hands and feet. Allow my heart to be open to the stories and lives of others, as you have taught them throughout their lives. Thank you for the personal narrative that you give each us and I praise you for the promise that all things work together for the good of those who are called according to your purposes, not mine (Rom. 8:28).

Barriers | Galatians 3:25-29

Runners have been breaking down barriers for hundreds of years now. People from all backgrounds gather together to run regardless of gender, race, or economic status. There is no space for discrimination when everyone is competing.

The early church was one of breaking down these barriers. Paul writes that all people are children of God! Not just the Jews, but the Gentiles too. Not just the men, but the women too. This would have been revolutionary in its time. The majority of the Jewish people were not very receptive to the message of Jesus, because it was so outwardly focused. It was not a message for the few, but for the masses.

There was nothing politically or socially correct about the movement of Jesus. He upset the status quo. His message is for the sick and hurting, the least of these—not the ones who have it all figured out.

Jesus was the beginning of an unprecedented movement that lives on despite his death and it thrives because of his resurrection. Similarly, runners are all about breaking records—doing things that have never been done before. We have the opportunity to take up our belongings and run the race as fiercely as he.

Lord, you have paved the way in breaking down the status quo. You sent your Son, fully man and fully divine, to earth to die the brutal death on the cross, but then he rose again. You are a mysterious, unpredictable, and life-enriching God who never ceases to amaze me. Thank you for the radical message of your Son that prompted the creation of the early church. I pray that I can embrace parts of this radical message to radically transform my life to look more like your Son's. Help me fix my eyes on Jesus, the creator and perfect example of my faith.

Slow Down | Matthew 6:5-13

Runners like results—fast times, improved times, top finishes. But to get results we know we must act quickly—wasting no time. So no time is wasted, we jump into things quickly.

Can you think of an example where you did something too quickly or too soon because you wanted immediate results? Think of jumping back into training too soon after nursing an injury (when a few more days of rest would have completely gotten rid of the pain). Or something as simple as starting a race unrealistically fast (then feeling like you hit a brick wall half way through). The examples I am thinking of are ones in which your intentions and heart may be in the right place, but the end result is not the best.

Let me bring you to the topic of prayer. Do you ever rush in and rush out prayer? Or say, "Hey! Let's just pray real quick!"

It's time to slow down. Often our intentions are right to take time to thank God or talk to him, but we rush through prayers or we get into the habit of saying the same words and phrases without even thinking about it.

One simple way to awaken a prayer to its true potential is for you to reevaluate who you are praying to. Stop and think. "Dear God." Wow. God. Creator of the Universe. Lover of my soul. Lord of my heart. Capable of anything. The God who sent his one and only Son that I may have eternal life. Now pause and take that in. Holy, Majestic and Mighty King. Stop and take in his presence before you say one more thing. Prepare your heart before the King. Humble yourself and offer your whole heart in prayer. You will begin to realize more of the love the Lord has for you each day as you embrace his greatness made perfect in your weakness.

Daily Training Thought: Rest

God created for six days and rested on the seventh (Gen. 2:2-3). If we are called to conform to the image of Christ and look towards his example, how are we supposed to rest?

Our bodies were not created for constant toil of the mind, body and soul. We do not need to conform to the stiffness of rabbinical teachings, because even Jesus stirred up trouble as he picked some heads of grain in the fields (Mark 2:23-28). But we do need to take moments of rest to offer a clear and empty heart to God so we may be filled.

We were not created to operate 40 hours straight. Humans were created as limited beings. Praise God for his divinity as the sun rises and the sun sets, giving us opportunities for new days with new rest. Our bodies recognize the limitation and submit to sleep.

All bodies were created differently so what does yours need for rest and rejuvenation? Let's not fool ourselves in thinking we are limitless.

Meditate on these verses:

"In peace I will lie down and sleep, for you alone, LORD, make me dwell in safety" (Psalm 4:8).

"So there remains a Sabbath rest for the people of God. For the one who has entered his rest has himself also rested from his works, as God did from his. Therefore be diligent to enter that rest, so that no one will fall, through following the same example of disobedience" (Hebrews 4:9-11).

Revival | Psalm 25:2-7

Are you familiar with the slump? The no good days that you drown yourself in your own pity? Perhaps it lasts a day. Sometimes we get caught in weeks or months of no improvement and begin to become discouraged.

Regardless, your attitude suffers from apathy and often results in discontentment toward yourself and others.

My prayer for you in these moments, days, and weeks is revival—revival of your mind and soul, and refreshment of your Spirit.

God is willing and ready to offer this gift to you, but are you ready to give it up? Are you ready to give up the slump and leave the apathy behind?

Be transformed by the renewing of your mind when you choose to surrender your weights of the world (Rom. 12:2). Don't get stuck on the little things that can bring you down, but lean on God who wants to bring you above your circumstances.

Holy Healer and Comforter, free me from the burdens of the world when its weight is heavy on my shoulders. I surrender all to you, God. In the good and in the bad, on the mountain and in the valley, save me from myself in any pride or foolishness. Renew my mind so I can serve you whole-heartedly with no reservations.

Paying the Price | Romans 3:21-26

Has someone covered your dinner bill before?

What if someone told you that they were going to pay for your running shoes as long as you need them? Or for all you road racers out there...what if someone told you that your race entry fees were covered for the rest of your life? They say, "Enjoy the races! No strings attached—just run free for the joy of running!"

How awesome would that be? You would be shocked and grateful. It would be difficult to not take this gift for granted after some time, forgetting how great this gift is.

The reality is that we have a debt that has been paid that FAR outweighs any of these examples. We have a Savior who paid the bill for our sin and purchased our freedom so we can have life and have it abundantly. You have freedom and it does not cost you anything, but obedience. Your life is no longer about what you have to do to repay this great sacrifice, but living out the beauty of what Christ has done for you.

Challenge: Look for opportunities to bless someone. While it feels good to receive, it is life changing to give. Take note of how it feels next time someone covers your bill or gives you a gift. Then, thank God for his sacrifice that covered your sin for all time. In fact, thank God constantly for his sacrifice. Don't let yourself take advantage of this gift.

Value | 1 Timothy 4:8-16

We understand how important bodily training is. In fact, the Bible affirms that it is valuable, but if physical training only holds *some* value, how much more value does godliness hold?

Godliness is not just important for this life like training is, but it also holds incredible value in the scheme of eternity. It does not just hold value for you, but it could make the difference for someone else.

When you are an ambassador of Christ, your resemblance of Christ may be the only reading of holiness that someone may see. Continue to edify yourself in speech, in conduct, in love, in faith, and in purity.

God, forgive me for giving priority to my running career when you are the one who should hold the greatest realm of importance in my life. Continuously teach me your ways as I seek you so I can make you the center of all I am and all I do.

Back to the Basics | Mark 12:28-34

Believe it or not, there is such a thing as overthinking a race or workout. Have you been there before? Have you worked yourself up and out of reality by getting in your own head?

A point arrives where you must simply run without all the details, just putting forth your heart and your body to do the work. When we become overwhelmed by the multitudes of minor details, we lose sight of the overall picture.

So often Christians get caught up in the legalistic laws of the faith and forget the big picture: Jesus Christ died to abolish the legalistic law and we are called to love God and love others. If we threw aside the legalism and began to focus on the bigger picture of selfless love, how would our world change?

What minor details do you need to leave aside today in order to focus on truly loving God and his people? Maybe it is time to forsake a bit of strategy and lead with your heart. We must walk a fine line and find balance in the details and the big picture. Pray that God would reveal that balance to you in all facets of your life.

Challenge: Focus on love today. For we should focus on "whatever is true, whatever is noble, whatever is right, whatever is pure, whatever is lovely, whatever is admirable--if anything is excellent or praiseworthy--think about such things" (Phil. 4:8). In moments of silence or idleness, do not reach for your phone or something to quickly occupy your mind. Instead focus on what love is. Praise God for his love.

"Love is patient, love is kind. It does not envy, it does not boast, it is not proud. It does not dishonor others, it is not self-seeking, it is not easily angered, it keeps no record of wrongs. Love does not delight in evil but rejoices with the truth. It always protects, always trusts, always hopes, always perseveres" (1 Corinthians 13:4-7).

Connected | John 15:1-17

In order to have success in your running career, training is essential. One must build up endurance and take care of the "little things" in order to be a better runner.

You put yourself through the grind: workouts, recovery runs, races, and cross training. You must be constantly in tune with your body and in tune with your training. The best runners are not distracted from their ambitions. If you lose touch with your training, you cannot expect improvement in your running.

We are bound and determined to not veer from the plan. We get in our workouts and runs if it's the last thing we will do. Yet sometimes it is so easy to veer away from God, even though this is of the utmost importance! You cannot lose touch with your Savior.

There are three principles I want you to evaluate if you or someone you know is feeling idle in spiritual growth:
1. Are you praying?
2. Are you reading/studying your Bible?
3. Are you fellowshipping with other believers?

You cannot expect to bear spiritual fruit if you are not rooted in God. It would be foolish to expect improvement if you were not training, so why do we expect spiritual growth when we are not seeking the Lord?

God, root me in your abounding love that is entirely unfathomable. Present me with a thirst and hunger for your Word that stretches and challenges me so I can more fully conform to the image of your Son. I pray that you would reveal to me opportunities to pray, read the Bible, and fellowship with others. I want more of you in my life, God.

All | Luke 9:21-27

Have you seen the t-shirt: "All give some, some give all"?

Running is measured in dedication. It is measured in how early you are up to run, how hard you are willing to go, and how much you are willing to sacrifice. The more you give means the more you get.

Let's contrast this with how much are you willing to sacrifice as a follower of Christ. Why is it so much more difficult to give all to something that holds eternal value? All Christians give some, but who do you know that gives all?

Do you know runners who give all to running? Do you know more people who sacrifice for running than for Christ and the church?

Are you willing to take the next step of surrender and give up your personal hopes and dreams for a lifestyle that serves beyond yourself? We often focus on the sacrifice of following Jesus rather than the joy. We do the opposite in our running and maybe that is why it is easier to sacrifice more.

We look to the potential joy in achieving our goals and the satisfaction of victory rather than the hard stuff along the way. Let's take our runner's mindset and begin to find the joy among the pain.

God, you offer me so much joy so forgive me for not realizing it. It is scary to surrender all to something I don't completely understand, but I pray that I can take the next steps towards you. Take an ounce of my dedication towards running and turn it into love for you each day. I believe you can transform my heart if I allow you to. Thank you, Lord.

Go | Matthew 9:9-13

In order for any results on the course or track to be produced, you have to get up and go. You have to answer the call of your training, because without a response nothing would happen.

Jesus believed the same thing. Jesus instructed his disciples to follow him and go out into the world. While actively pursuing the kingdom, Jesus's disciples did not stop, sit, or even wait. There was no passive pursuit of the gospel.

Jesus did not tell Matthew to continue on with what he was doing, but he told him to follow. So Matthew got up and went. The kingdom requires vibrant movement! We are not called to live the same lives that we lived before Jesus. There should be a noticeable difference in the way we talk, act, and react.

Jesus sent *out* his disciples as he issued the Great Commission. Kingdom work happens when we are living dynamically—we should be actively following, seeking, loving and being the hands and feet of Jesus.

God, thank you for giving me the desire to be physically active as I run and pursue physical fitness. I understand all the more how important movement is in my life. Help me take the principles of running and movement that I exercise every day and apply them to my relationship with you. I want to take my discipline, perseverance and desire to be active and apply it an exciting, deep, passionate relationship with you. I am ready for this next step, God! Take me and all that I have to offer.

Conclusion

Gospel

This is the good news of Jesus Christ who lived a perfect life as a Jewish man that was fully man and a fully divine. He was born into this earth with a purpose. That purpose was to save us from separation. The separation between God and man.

This separation began at the beginning of the time in the ever-so familiar Garden of Eden. After being tempted by Satan, Adam and Eve made a choice to seek the ways of the world as they sought their own will above the Lord's. They chose the one tree in the Garden that God told them was forbidden. We often forget that God gave them the freedom to choose from any other tree that would have fulfilled them in him. Instead they pursued the same fate that we still pursue today: control and power over our own lives. We call this "The Fall" (Gen. 3).

While Adam and Eve were cut off from the Garden, God did not stop pursuing his people. History is the story of God's endless pursuit of the human heart.

There is one thing that God cannot control and that is the heart. If God wanted robots, he could have programmed everyone to love him, but he loves us enough to give us the choice. So he gave us our hearts and his will is for us to seek him, because we will not find fulfillment any place else.

Throughout the Old Testament, God guided his people in hopes they would find him and be satisfied. Trial and error. Praise and defeat. The people of Israel could not pursue God with pure hearts. God requires perfection, because he is perfection and this separation between God and man could not be bridged. So that is when Jesus Christ came onto the scene.

God decided to send his Son in the likeness of man to redeem all of creation and announce the coming of his kingdom.

While Jesus was on earth, he preached of a kingdom that was here, but not quite yet. This doesn't exactly make sense until you read and explore his message (Luke 17:20-25).

The kingdom was for everyone, not just the Jewish people. A Heavenly King rules this kingdom and all the nations would submit to his perfect will; then, there would be absolute harmony in all the world.

Jesus preached this message (Luke 8:1) which was threatening to the Roman Empire at the time and radical in the context of the Jewish people also.

As was predicted by the prophets and Jesus himself, he was betrayed and crucified on the cross. Jesus was perfection. He not only fulfilled the Jewish law perfectly, but he gave it depth and life application. Murder is not only wrong, but hating your brother is just as bad (1 John 3:15)!

Jesus was fully man and he fulfilled the perfection that the Father so deeply longed for (Hebrews 4:15). But if God was going to forgive his people from their sin for all time, Jesus also needed to bear the weight of this sin or this imperfection. If our God is indeed just, he must punish for what is not pure according to his will; therefore, he poured out his wrath on his Son and Jesus was separated from God. But this is only part one of the story.

The good news is that three days later, Jesus rose (1 Cor. 15:3-6). The righteous requirement of the perfect law was fulfilled in Jesus Christ (Rom. 8:4), because the grave was conquered. No more sacrifices needed to be offered, but Jesus was the ultimate sacrifice as God's wrath was satisfied on the cross (Heb. 10:1-8). If Jesus wouldn't have risen from the dead, there would be no gospel.

God is ruling and reigning in the kingdom that continues to spread across the world. We can be a part of this kingdom when we accept the truth of Jesus' life, death and resurrection.

IV

Salvation in Jesus is often mistaken for "fire insurance"—a going to heaven pass. Eternal life in Jesus Christ is not just life after death, but life right now. Jesus does not preach on how to get to heaven, but how to live so that the kingdom of God is spread to all corners of the earth.

Life is more than a passing pleasure or drudgery—it is everything as it has been given and guided by God in accordance to his will once Jesus Christ is accepted as the Lord and King of life (Eph. 2:6-10).

God does not want you for your good deeds. God can do good deeds on the earth. There are plenty of people who are willing and ready to do good. God wants your heart submitted in all joy and love. From the beginning of time, God has been after the human heart because *he* wants to love and satisfy the limitless desires of your soul. There is not mutual joy in loving someone without being loved back. God is waiting for your love so he can pour out his abundant love, grace, and forgiveness on your life (Jas. 4:8). He wants to give you all of this in eternal life that starts as soon as you embrace him in light of his Son and his kingdom.

Read the whole story of Jesus Christ in Matthew, Mark, Luke, or John for the full gospel.

V

Now What?

Surrender.

Today is the best day to give it over to the Lord.

You know better than anyone that you cannot do this on your own. If you haven't already, you need to find a community of believers to plug in with. Find a local church or Bible study and continue to seek God's will for your life personally. You seek God's will by walking in his ways; these ways are laid out in his Word.

Log onto www.facebook.com/SpiritualRunner to leave feedback, communicate with others, and see how God is working through Spiritual Runners.

If you have ideas to expand God's reach through runners or have a message to share, email me at SpiritualRunner4Him @gmail.com.

Spiritual Runner Vision

I pray that this book will be the starting point for a great movement in the running community. I pray this book will prompt questions which eventually result in faithful growth and a life of fulfillment in Christ.

There are so many people that are "good people" who are on fire with a love of running. I believe these people could change everything if they embraced the message of Jesus Christ. He is just like us—not the church-going boy that our culture has made him out to be.

Running teaches on so many faith-related topics as runners learn in endurance, victory, training, defeat, perseverance, accountability, honoring your body, community, etc. We can take all of these disciplines and change the world in light of the radical message and love of Jesus Christ.

Long term, I would love to meet with runners in camps, conferences and retreats to build upon these disciplines and send runners out to all ends of the earth.

I truly believe we have a unique opportunity to turn today's Christianity on its head and "seek first the kingdom" (Matt. 6:33).

Acknowledgements

This book was written in stages:

Inspired in June of 2011. On and off again through the running seasons. Convinced I had a publisher in 2012. Decided not. God tapped me on the shoulder too many times to ignore, so I started writing again. Went on a life-changing semester abroad trip in the Middle East where I found myself inspired to finish and publish.

My heart was stirred and spurred on by the Lord to start and complete this project and he deserves all the glory. I praise him for the way he has used his faithful children to encourage me in my pursuit of him. My faith has been strengthened through trials and by dozens of people whose stories have inspired me to breathe more life into the kingdom that God has brought about.

My family and my best friend Molly.

My coaches. They have each taught me *so* much about running and those lessons have rolled over into my life on so many occasions.

My teammates throughout my high school and college years. Words cannot say how much I have learned from each of you as we have experienced all emotions in victory and defeat.

My running buddies, the Montreat XC camp, FCA and the running community as a whole who loves, supports, and radiates passion which has *truly* inspired me in writing this.

Bethany Hench for this awesome cover.

Notes

1."Worship" *Merriam-Webster.com*. 2014. http://www.merriam-webster.com (6 May 2014).

2. Greear, JD. Gospel: Recovering the Power that Made Christianity Revolutionary. Nashville: B&H Publishing Group, 2011.

3. United Church of God. The Different Kinds of Love Mentioned in the Bible. May 2014. <http://www.ucg.org/booklet/marriage-and-family-missing-dimension/divorce-proof-your-marriage/different-kinds-love-menti/>.

4. Grace Communion International. What is Worship? May 2014. <http://www.gci.org/God/worship>.

CPSIA information can be obtained
at www.ICGtesting.com
Printed in the USA
LVOW03s1255120617
537815LV00033B/1563/P